Crush the British Foe

Korea: A Spiritual Factor

April 29—The stunning process which has become most visible in Korea over the past days—and how many were there who expected this even just weeks ago?—is still far from the complete victory for which we are fighting. So far, it is still only an embattled outpost. The British-led attack on Syria two weeks ago was aimed to prevent this progress; it damaged it severely, and next time, if we permit a next time, can be much more harmful.

But even as an embattled outpost, the hope which the Korea talks represent, has nevertheless swept the world with its inspiration. It was perfectly natural that the thousands of supporters at President Trump's Michigan rally on April 28 began to chant "No-bel," "No-bel!" when he mentioned Korea. Regardless of party or faction, there is no one with any shred of understanding and morality, who can fail to find some degree of inspiration from the Korea deveolopments today. Recall that the state of declared hostilities on the Korean Peninsula has existed ever since 1950, when the world's population was only 2.5 billion, as against 7.6 billion today. And only about 7% of those alive today, had even been born when that never-ending war began. And that the Korean War inaugurated that Cold War which dominated the remainder of the terrible 20th Century. Equally today, the frozen Korea conflict still underpins the British Imperial system of pitting each against all to sustain its world rule.

What is now first unfolding in Korea has been made possible by the joint and coordinated work of China, Japan, Russia, and the United States with the two Koreas. What has finally permitted this, is that China, Japan, Russia, and the United States have all undergone profound changes over the recent decades, which only now made this form of cooperation possible today, where it had never been possible before. What caused these changes? The new policies of Presidents Xi, Putin, Trump, and Prime Minister Abe? Yes, but what was in common to all of them?

There is a spiritual factor. As Douglas MacArthur wisely said aboard the battleship *Missouri* in Tokyo Bay, "It must be of the spirit if we are to save the flesh." Lyndon LaRouche referenced this in his seminal 2004 work, "The Coming Eurasian World," where he wrote, "What occurs, as I have seen thus often, even at close quarters, in the course of my lifetime, the evolution of the collective mind of an entire culture, is driven by the spark of the interventions into the entire society, through the veil of ambiguity, by a relatively few geniuses, and by those young people who replicate experience of discovery by geniuses in their own early self-development through young adulthood." See http://www.larouchepub.com/eiw/public/2004/eirv31n49-20041217/eirv31n49-20041217_004-toward_a_second_treaty_of_westph-lar.pdf

The "Coming Eurasian World," the next great phase of human evolution of which Lyndon LaRouche prophesied there, is now coming into view, driven by the sparks of genius which he has scattered through many decades. The Korean talks vouchsafe us that it is possible, that it can be done. Now it stands out clearly before us, like the New World to Schiller's Columbus. Will we realize it now?

EIRContents

www.larouchepub.com   Volume 45, Number 18, May 4, 2018

ZEPP-LAROUCHE WEBCAST

London-Based Empire Exposed: Door Open for Trans-Atlantic Economic Change

This is the edited transcript of the April 26, 2018 Schiller Institute New Paradigm webcast, an interview with the founder of the Schiller Institutes, Helga Zepp-LaRouche. She was interviewed by Harley Schlanger. A video of the webcast is available.

Harley Schlanger: Hello. I'm Harley Schlanger with the Schiller Institute. Welcome to this week's international webcast featuring our founder and chairman Helga Zepp-LaRouche.

We're entering a very intense period of diplomatic activity, much of it related to the advances of the New Silk Road, although regrettably some of it is related to efforts to enforce the old rules of the old paradigm. I think we should start with a report from Germany this week by a parliamentary organization, on the illegality of the April 9 missile attack on Syria by the United States, the United Kingdom, and France. Helga, what is the committee that put out this report, and what did it say?

Helga Zepp-LaRouche: It is the Scientific Research Service (*Wissenschaftlichen Dienste*), staffed by experts who advise *Bundestag* members on various issues. The Scientific Research Service was asked to issue an opinion on the legality of these military strikes against Syria. The

opinion concluded that the missile attacks constitute a violation of international law. I think it's very important to discuss that, because Chancellor Merkel said that these strikes were "necessary and appropriate," and Germany's Defense Minister, Ursula von der Leyen, said it's a shame that Germany was not part of it, and added, we weren't asked this time, but that in the future,

Witnesses of the supposed chemical attack in Douma, Syria including 11-year-old Hassan Diab (shown here) and hospital staff, told reporters at The Hague that the White Helmets video was staged.

Germany would like to play a role on a global scale in similar functions.

The Scientific Research Service reported that that military action, which was not sanctioned by the UN Security Council, is an example of a practice that replaces the principle of legality with the principle of subjective moral legitimacy; that this is actually in the tradition of the gunboat diplomacy before World War I, and also between the World Wars. It was the horrors of World War II which then caused the international community to establish the presently existing international law, as reflected in the UN Charter and similar documents.

To abandon that body of law and go back to a pre-World War I mode of arbitrary military strikes by nations creates a very, very dangerous precedent. Other jurists who commented on it, said that by the same token, any state can attack, copying that model and proclaiming that it has some beef with its neighbors, and conduct similar military strikes, in which case you end up in a completely uncontrollable situation that could quickly lead to a new world war.

I would really like you, our audience, to focus on this point. International law, as discussed in this report, is something extremely precious, and we must not abandon it. This military strike would have been completely illegal for Germany to participate in, because Article 26 of the *Grundgesetz*, the Basic Law of Germany, prohibits the preparation of a war of aggression. Whoever violates that law could be subject to a life sentence in prison.

These strikes also violate a UN General Assembly Resolution, dating back to 1974, that defines a war of aggression as a "crime against international peace." It is very important that we not allow the world to drift into a might-makes-right lawless situation in which we live by the law of the jungle, the brutal concept of the survival of the fittest. This is a very dangerous path to follow. We must remind ourselves what wars of aggression lead to.

The Scientific Research Service also noted that this military strike was done even before the Organization for the Prohibition of Chemical Weapons (OPCW) had made known their findings, aggravating this case as a

Syria airstrikes violated international law: German parliamentary report

The German government supported the airstrikes by the US, UK and France in response to an alleged chemical weapons attack. But a new report has said the airstrikes infringed upon international law.

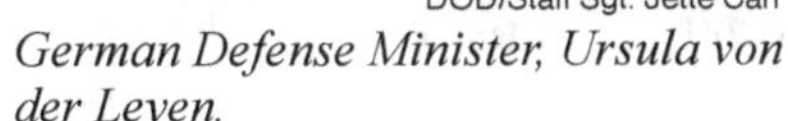

DOD/Staff Sgt. Jette Carr

German Defense Minister, Ursula von der Leyen.

Xinhua/Ye Pingfan

German Chancellor Angela Merkel.

violation of international law.

Let me emphasize this point. It is very unfortunate that President Trump got pulled into this military strike. There is the danger that if this is allowed to pass without the proper international review, a repetition of such a military act outside the bounds of international law, could get much worse and go out of control. Such a danger absolutely exists. I would like you to help us to sharpen the awareness of such a danger. It should be taken up by the United Nations, based on that Resolution from 1974, which defines a war of aggression as a crime against international peace. I would like you to really give some thought to it. Don't just say, "OK, we'll just do these things," because there are consequences which could mean, in the final analysis, the end of civilization.

Schlanger: There was a report on German television that raised questions about the so-called chemical attack in Syria. Is this going to have any effect in the *Bundestag*? Is there much discussion of this now, as a result of this report?

Zepp-LaRouche: Well, it's another classical example of what happens. One courageous, or just objective journalist, Uli Gack, the head of Germany's national public television channel (ZDF) office in Cairo, reported from Syria that he had spoken to many witnesses in and around Douma and they all told him that there was no chemical weapons use by the government, that it was rather a typical provocation from the jihadists. In this same program, broadcast during the prime time news slot, Gack quoted British journalist Robert Fisk from the *Independent*, who had already made a similar observation which was published in that newspaper.

So then, all hell broke loose. ZDF, the official TV channel, distanced itself from this report. *Bildzeitung* and *Focus* magazine attacked the broadcast by Gack, calling it conspiracy theory. ZDF clamped down on Gack and forced him to not pursue this story any further. These other media accused a prominent mainstream journalist—actually one of the more honest journalists—of being a conspiracy theorist. It's a complete, classical example of the kind of *Gleichschaltung* [enforced conformity] in the Western mainstream media these days.

This is *not* the end of the story. The OPCW fact-finding mission has returned to Syria, and I think tomorrow there will be a meeting of the OPCW in The Hague, where the Russians will bring several new Syrian witnesses to testify on what they saw. We know what earlier witnesses had said: There was shouting by the jihadists about chemical weapons. Then they did the filming and *nothing* was happening, except this staged scenario.

This is not the end of the story. Unless the truth of this fraudulent report of a chemical attack is uncovered, the danger of a repetition is absolutely there.

Schlanger: Let's stick with Syria for a moment because it's such a crucial issue. French President Em-

French President Emmanuel Macron, addressing a joint meeting of the U.S. Congress, April 25, 2018.

manuel Macron is on a state visit to the United States. He is continuing to pull out all the stops, to try to manipulate President Trump into committing the United States to keep troops in Syria. What is it that Macron is doing? Why is he taking the point on this, Helga?

Zepp-LaRouche: The policy is actually the British policy. Macron is not doing himself any favors by being the spearhead of that British policy. I think he has an idea of positioning himself as the leader of the European Union. He gave a speech to a Joint Session of Congress, which was absolutely terrible and not toned down at all, given that he got a standing ovation from members of the U.S. Congress. That speech was in sharp contrast to the discussion he had before the speech with Trump, which you referenced. Macron attacked unilateralism and nationalism, all of which was aimed at Trump's policies, getting the support of the Democrats and the neo-cons and so forth.

I don't think this will necessarily stick. The problem is that Trump *does* change his views, sometimes rather quickly. However, I was told that Trump reiterated that the aim of U.S. policy is to get out of Syria as quickly as possible after ISIS is defeated—this reiteration being after Macron left. So I don't necessarily think that Macron succeeded. Even so, it was very clear that Macron was fully on the geopolitical old paradigm line, and was also trying to bypass and outflank German Chancellor Angela Merkel, who is arriving today for a visit of several hours with Trump at the White House tomorrow.

Macron's intervention was terrible. One can only hope that Trump won't be influenced by it, but is looking forward to his upcoming summit with President Putin, which is much, much more important than the policy of the European Union. Macron in Washington, D.C. also spoke about the initiation of a new grouping that is supposed to create a bridge between the Geneva process and the Astana process of peace negotiations in Syria. What we have seen in some of the conferences on the reconstruction of Syria is that neither the United States nor the EU is giving *any* money for the reconstruction of Syria as such, but only for those areas which are not under the control of the Assad government. So that tells you a lot about the European attitude towards Syria. Regime change against the Assad government is still the policy, and that is very terrible, very bad.

India and China

Schlanger: U.S. Ambassador to Moscow Jon Huntsman issued a statement reiterating that President Trump is seeking a détente policy with Russia, and is very much looking forward to the meeting with Putin.

On the other hand, we're seeing a whole series of initiatives around the New Silk Road perspective, starting with the April 24 Council of Foreign Ministers of the Shanghai Cooperation Organization (SCO) meeting in Beijing. The SCO Heads of State Council Meeting is coming up on June 9-10 in China.

I'd like to get to get your thoughts on other activity, between India and China—Indian Prime Minister Modi is going to China next week—and between Japan and China. There's a lot going on. What do you make of all this, Helga?

Zepp-LaRouche: These are very important developments. I spoke to some of my friends in India earlier today for their assessment. There is clearly a recognition that after the border crisis in Doklam, between China and India, last year, there is a recognition that it is much more in the interests of the two countries to work together. Now, I think this is very good, because

PID

Indian Prime Minister Modi (left) and Chinese President Xi Jinping, April 28, 2018.

there was a danger that Modi would make his next election campaign on an anti-China profile. But there will be a summit in Wuhan between Xi Jinping and Narendra Modi, starting April 27.

Professor Zhang Jiadong of Fudan University commented on this in a very interesting way. He said that India and China are the only two countries that belong to the club of nations that have more than 1 billion people; that together they represent 40 percent of the world's population. They both have continuous, 5,000-year histories. They have produced many contributions to world civilization, and when they work together, being the two largest countries on the planet, this is of extreme importance.

Chinese Foreign Minister Wang Yi announced that Xi Jinping and Modi will discuss developments which occur only once in a century. And while I'm not sure what he means exactly by that, I think what he is referring to is the epochal changes of strategic alignment which are going on in Asia right now, and that is what President Xi Jinping is trying to accomplish also with the upcoming SCO Heads of State Council meeting on June 9-10—after the Belt and Road Initiative and the BRICS association, now the SCO—that all of this is supposed to lead to a completely new model of international relations, what Xi Jinping always calls the "shared community for the one future of mankind."

Given the clear rapprochement between Japan and China, and between Japan and Russia, you can see that all of these Asian countries are seeking a better way. There are still some obstacles, such as the issue between India and Pakistan, which I don't think has been resolved, and India's opposition to the China-Pakistan Economic Corridor, also not yet resolved; but these countries are moving toward each other. A very interesting comment in a Chinese news article said that the relations between China and Japan could now be modeled,— or you could use the parallel of the European Coal and Steel Community in the beginning of the 1950s, when France gave the olive branch to Germany just five years after the end of the Second World War.

Adm. Philip Davidson, U.S. Pacific Fleet Commander.

This is a reference to the past war experience between China and Japan: If Germany and France were able to settle their problems of world war in that way, so can China and Japan.

I think this is going in a very, very good direction. It shows you one thing very clearly: that the future of civilization is in Asia, and any country of the West that wants to be part of that future, should find a good relationship to this new dynamic, because this is the forward-looking one, and not the old paradigm as represented by some of these European powers that just think in terms of the past.

Schlanger: Your husband Lyndon LaRouche emphasized many, many years ago, that an India-China-Russia relationship, which could naturally include the United States, would be the basis for establishing something totally new in the world.

Helga, you've travelled to India and China a number of times; you've met with leaders in both countries. Is there anything that you can see that would get in the way of an improved relationship? Isn't now, really, the time for this to happen?

Zepp-LaRouche: It's a strategic necessity for the Asian countries to work together. Unfortunately, Adm. Philip Davidson, the replacement for Adm. Harry Harris as commander of the U.S. Pacific Command, has just delivered a blood-curdling attack on Russia and China, and accused China of all kinds of things at his confirmation hearings in the Senate Armed Services Committee. So the geopolitical thinking is not yet gone. One could say that this idea of a China-Russia-India alliance was actually furthered by the behavior of the neo-cons, the Iraq War, the Afghanistan intervention, and the Libya attack; so I think these countries have moved together much more quickly than they normally would have done, as a result of these policies of the Bush-Obama-Blair-Cameron-May kind of policies.

You can always have a terrible incident. Remember the Gulf of Tonkin incident which was spun into a war escalation. Some new pretext could be created to cause a new crisis. This is why the legality of these military strikes against Syria needs to be discussed internationally. The intention of the Chinese and Russian leadership—and now hopefully also that of India and Japan—is to move into a New Paradigm. The New Silk Road Spirit has caught on. The countries of Asia have understood that this is the moment in history in which we need a completely new set of relations if mankind is to get into safe waters and have a bright future.

I am optimistic, I'm very optimistic. Tomorrow's summit between Kim Jong-un and President Moon Jae-in of South Korea also looks very good. If it's any reflection, the President of the International Olympic Committee, Thomas Bach, said that in his talks with the South Korean and North Korean governments, they both expressed the intention to join the next Olympics and to again have a joint team. Based on his discussions, he's extremely optimistic about the intention of these two governments.

So if you look at all of these developments, I think it is actually very good. Some of these geopoliticians probably will never change, because they cannot imagine that mankind can grow out of the old kind of pettiness and rivalry and competition, that a New Paradigm of win-win cooperation is actually possible. But if the majority of mankind is moving in this direction, I'm very confident and hopeful that this New Paradigm will prevail.

Schlanger: President Trump had a little bit of fun with this, when he made fun of the media for saying that

North Korean leader Kim Jong-un (left) with South Korean President Moon Jae-in on the red carpet outside the Peace House in Panmunjom during the elaborate welcoming ceremony for their historic meeting on April 27, 2018.

there would never be any progress with North Korea, telling them, "Look, you don't know what's going to happen—it may not work," but he's very happy with the response from Kim Jong-un. He has just sent a team including the top trade officials to China to discuss the trade agreement. And what he said, which I think shapes their outlook, is that he has great respect for Xi Jinping and a great friendship. Do you have any thoughts on what might happen with these discussions going on between the United States and China?

Zepp-LaRouche: That's difficult, because on the Chinese side is Vice Premier Liu He, the most important economic advisor of Xi Jinping. Liu has just recently been elevated to the Politburo and the State Council; he will represent the potential of the Belt and Road Initiative. On the side of the American delegation, for sure will be Treasury Secretary Steven Mnuchin. We have criticized him and also U.S. Trade Representative Robert Lighthizer for not being aligned with Trump's election promises. However, Mnuchin had, at one point, made mention of the American System.

I don't know. I imagine that China will propose the way to overcome the trade deficit, in the way Foreign Minister Wang Yi and also Prime Minister Li Keqiang have suggested—namely that, other than tariffs, you could also increase the trade between the two countries, and have joint ventures in third countries, and in that

way, reduce the trade deficit by just increasing the trade. I imagine that the Chinese will reiterate this proposal. How these two, or four, delegates from the United States—it's not so clear—will respond; we don't know. One can only hope they recognize the potential that American industries would benefit greatly from participating in such joint ventures in third countries along the Belt and Road. U.S.-Chinese relations could also benefit a lot, if the United States were to allow Chinese investments in the buildup of U.S. infrastructure.

We will have to see how that develops. I'm optimistic that the Chinese will not miss the opportunity to make such proposals. That is why the Schiller Institute is so important. We are making these ideas more known inside the United States, so that more and more people will be able to recognize the potential that lies in U.S.-China cooperation in the Belt and Road Initiative. So, you should join the Schiller Institute and help us to make these ideas more known.

Warnings from the U.S. Federal Reserve Bank

Schlanger: We do know there's support for expansion of U.S.-China trade in Alaska and West Virginia, as well other states, and from cities, notably Houston, Texas—delegations have travelled from the United States to China, and from China to the United States, to talk about specific investments.

We are talking about investments, but we should never lose sight of the financial crisis. Behind the strategic confrontation is the collapse of this financial system that is being held together by unbelievable amounts of new funny-money and fake credit that is continuing to build up an ever increasing, unpayable debt bubble.

Helga, there were more warnings recently coming out of the U.S. Federal Reserve Bank by a couple of officials. There's talk about an interest rate problem, a shake-up at Deutsche Bank. What do you see in the financial picture? It's really quite shaky. It seems like now is the time for a new concerted effort around your husband's four basic laws.

Zepp-LaRouche: We are sitting on a strategic powder keg. One of the three governors of the Federal Reserve is already warning that the wave of corporate insolvencies, which have increased over last year by 60 percent, is so severe that it could cause a new banking

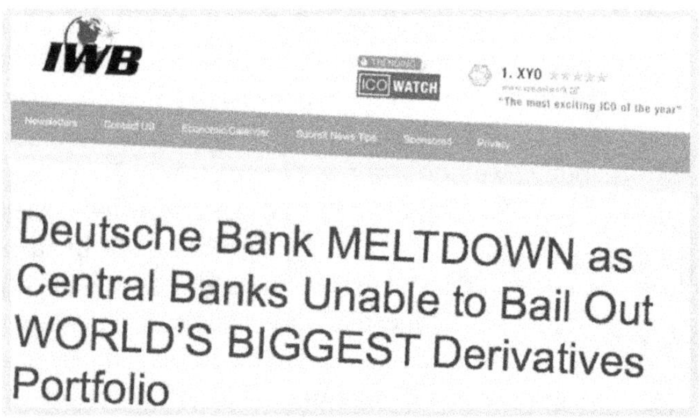

Deutsche Bank MELTDOWN as Central Banks Unable to Bail Out WORLD'S BIGGEST Derivatives Portfolio

crisis. The Fed is not known to make alarmist statements; they generally use a language to calm down the markets and respect the so-called "psychology of the markets." So if such a warning is coming from the Federal Reserve, it should be taken quite seriously.

There are also news articles about Deutsche Bank. The IMF called Deutsche Bank the riskiest bank in the world. It has $42 trillion in derivatives contracts outstanding! Some of these contracts balance each other out, so it may not be $42 trillion, but this is 15 times Germany's annual GDP, so this is not a small amount. One day we could all wake up—or in the middle of the day—and have a complete repetition of 2008, but on a much larger scale.

We need the Four Laws of my husband, Lyndon LaRouche, with the emphasis—not only on Glass-Steagall, and a National Bank and credit system—but an emphasis especially on the fourth law. Unless you have a complete push for innovation and qualitative breakthroughs in applying new universal principles in the economic platform, as my husband has discussed it in many of his writings, you will not pull out of the terrible shape the economies of the trans-Atlantic system are in, especially in the United States, Southern Europe— there are some real problem cases. An emphasis must be placed on such projects as thermonuclear fusion, space cooperation, and the application of the most advanced new physical principles in the economy, if you want to save the situation.

There is no discussion about that idea of applying new universal physical principles going on in Europe or in the United States at all. Let us really emphasize this and escalate the mobilization for the implementation of these Four Laws, not only in the United States, but also in Europe. The country which is closest to it is China: Xi Jinping has just met with an economic group, and, again emphasized the need to warn and safeguard China against financial risk. China is de-emphasizing any kind of speculative activity. Wall Street and the City of London are very far from using such an application of reason in their practices.

Schlanger: I was just reviewing some reports over the last couple of days on this. One of the things that many economists do acknowledge, is that with all the pep talk about how great the economy is doing, there is wage stagnation and the lowest labor participation level in four decades. They also always come back to productivity: There are no productivity gains.

As you just said, the Chinese clearly have a sense of what happened with the United States with NASA under John Kennedy. The Chinese space program today is oriented toward the highest technology; their rail system, the same thing; and so on. It seems as though this should be a no-brainer for people in the United States, just to look at our own history and realize that this works.

To reiterate what Helga Zepp-LaRouche said: The Schiller Institute is mobilizing internationally for the Four Laws, and especially at this point in time, we need to get President Trump to go back to his thinking during his campaign, both about the alliance with Russia and China, and also about support for Glass-Steagall and a real infrastructure program.

We've seen the U.S. Congress completely botch any effort by the President to get an infrastructure plan going. Wouldn't getting such an infrastructure plan underway be a winning strategy for anybody going into the 2018 election?

Zepp-LaRouche: I think that the dynamic taking place in Asia right now will shape history for the better. I'm absolutely convinced that what is happening between China and Africa, China and Latin America, China and Eurasia, is shaping history to the benefit of all of mankind. Many European nations are already completely onboard the New Silk Road development in terms of infrastructure. This includes the East European, Central European countries, Balkans, Italy, Spain, Portugal, Austria, Switzerland—all of these countries— even Belgium and Holland, the Scandinavian countries. They all have all recognized the great potential in the infrastructure cooperation of the New Silk Road.

Right now, the biggest problem in some countries, such as Germany and the United States, is that the mass media have not done justice to what is actually happening. This is the largest infrastructure program in history. Some people are debating whether it's 12 times or 20 times the size of the Marshall Plan—remember it's open ended! It will completely transform the planet. Our vision, as presented in the book, *The New Silk Road Becomes the World Land-Bridge*, is being realized by the majority of nations at a rapid pace.

Some people are trying to continue to play the old geopolitical games, saying the New Silk Road is just an effort by China to take over the world. First of all, it's not true. All these countries are happy to overcome poverty, underdevelopment. Why not? That is why they are so engaged with China in developing the New Silk Road.

The biggest problem is that the average person in Europe and the United States does not know the scope of these positive changes taking place in the world right now. I can only say, help us to spread these ideas. We, all of humanity, are facing a test: If we allow NATO to continue to move right up to the Russian border, if we continue to escalate the arms race—which is still a danger given that the new commander of the U.S. Pacific Command, Philip Davidson, has just said that China is ahead in certain areas, and so now the United States must catch up, with hypersonic weapons, and cyber weapons, and whatnot—as a civilization, we might not survive. We have to get rid of that kind of thinking.

Think about it. The previous administrations of the United States wasted $7 trillion on wars in the Middle East and North Africa that have brought nothing but misery. These wars caused millions of deaths and created a refugee crisis. Why not think about investing that kind of money in infrastructure, in education, and all that benefits the common good? Give people a sense of the future and hope. Inspire young people such that they will not want to destroy their minds in this drug epidemic, not be driven to commit suicide or the other acts of violence we are experiencing at increasing rates. Don't you think it's time that mankind must really move into a new Renaissance and work together as a human species?

Let us reach out to more countries and more layers of people in the countries of the West, to understand what this New Silk Road Spirit is all about.

Again, join the Schiller Institute and help us to spread these ideas.

Schlanger: Helga, I think you just made it very clear. Thanks for joining us this week, and we'll see you next week.

Zepp-LaRouche: Yes, till next week.

The New Silk Road Becomes the World Land-Bridge

The BRICS countries have a strategy to prevent war and economic catastrophe. It's time for the rest of the world to join!

This 374-page report is a road-map to the New World Economic Order that Lyndon and Helga LaRouche have championed for over 20 years.

Includes:

Introduction by Helga Zepp-LaRouche, "The New Silk Road Leads to the Future of Mankind!"

The metrics of progress, with emphasis on the scientific principles required for survival of mankind: nuclear power and desalination; the fusion power economy; solving the water crisis.

The three keystone nations: China, the core nation of the New Silk Road; Russia's mission in North Central Eurasia and the Arctic; India prepares to take on its legacy of leadership.

Other regions: The potential contributions of Southwest, Central, and Southeast Asia, Australia, Europe, and Africa.

The report is available in PDF $35 and in hard copy $50 (softcover) $75 (hardcover)
plus shipping and handling.
Order from http://store.larouchepub.com

The Science of Profit Is The Profit of Science

by Susan Kokinda

April 28—"Ford Retreats from American Car Business in Penny-Pinching Push," and "Ford Just Killed the Car" read newspaper headlines on April 26, 2018. The decision by Ford Motor Company to discontinue its lineup of sedans in favor of SUVs, crossovers, trucks, and, of course, the quintessential baby-boomer fantasy car—the Mustang, was driven by the desire to increase profits. But more significant than the shakeup in the product line, was the further announcement that there would be cuts in engineering, materials costs, and sales and marketing. The company expects to spend $5 billion less between 2019 and 2022 than previously planned in capital expenditures. All this is occurring under the tenure of James Hackett, the turn-around specialist, who was appointed CEO one year ago, replacing Mark Fields who, despite generating solid profits, was not making the stockholders or "the market" happy enough.

A few days earlier, LaRouche PAC policy committee member Bill Roberts, speaking to a meeting of supporters in the Detroit area, challenged the audience to think about profit from Lyndon LaRouche's standpoint, asserting that the only legitimate source of profit is science, and that profit cannot be measured from the standpoint of money, but rather from the standpoint of increases in physical production which derive from scientific advances.

Roberts used the example of Henry Ford (whose modern day company "just killed the car") in buying out the Dodge brothers and other stockholders, so that he could reinvest the profits of the Ford Motor Company to build the River Rouge complex in Dearborn, the largest industrial complex in the world, rather than paying out fat dividends. The Rouge plant was started just seven years after

the construction of the Highland Park plant, which housed the first automobile assembly line. Obviously the capital expenditures of Highland Park had not yet been recovered, and yet there was Ford, building something huge and new—a facility which ultimately employed 100,000 workers.

The contrast between monetary profit and true scientific profit reflects the challenge of presenting Lyndon LaRouche's "Four New Laws to Save the USA Now," issued in 2014. Excerpting those introductory sections which LaRouche himself highlighted, we have the injunction for the federal government to—

institute four specific, cardinal measures: measures which must be fully consistent with the specific intent of the original U.S. Federal Con-

Ford Media Center

Bill Ford, Jr., executive chairman, Ford Motor Company (left) and Jim Hackett, president and chief executive officer, unveil the all-new Ford Ranger at the 2018 North American International Auto Show.

Re-enact Glass-Steagall: *Franklin D. Roosevelt signs Glass-Steagall Act, 1933.*

National Banking: *Hamilton's First Bank of the United States (1797-1811).*

Infrastructure: *Norris Dam constructed by FDR's Tennessee Valley Authority.*

Fusion-Driver Program: *National Spherical Torus Experiment (NSTX) facility.*

stitution, as had been specified by U.S. Treasury Secretary Alexander Hamilton while he remained in office:

(1) Immediate re-enactment of the Glass-Steagall law instituted by U.S. President Franklin D. Roosevelt, without modification, as to principle of action.

(2) A return to a system of top-down, and thoroughly defined, National Banking....

(3) The purpose of the use of a Federal Credit-system, is to generate high-productivity trends in improvements of employment, with the accompanying intention, to increase the physical-economic productivity, and the standard of living of the persons and households of the United States....

(4) Adopt a Fusion-Driver "Crash Program." The essential distinction of man from all lower forms of life, hence, in practice, is that it presents the means for the perfection of the spe-cifically affirmative aims and needs of human individual and social life.

But Americans are so contaminated by the language of money, it is often difficult to discuss those four laws in the order written. Take the first. Mention of Glass-Steagall often prompts the question, "Why don't we have Glass-Steagall yet?" Why, indeed? President Trump is for it, Bernie Sanders is for it. Both the Democratic and Republican parties put it in their 2016 platforms. So why don't we have it?

Glass-Steagall will never be reinstated by people who see it merely as a reform of a rotten Wall Street-dominated monetary system. And most of its champions and supporters view it that way. To the contrary, Lyndon LaRouche has always fought for it as an action necessary to restore and protect a commercial banking sector which exists within an economic system based on a principle entirely opposed to Wall Street's monetarism and speculation. It is not a question of trying to rein in speculation; it is an intention rather to destroy monetarism and those principles which foster it.

Similarly, discussions of a National Bank often prompt, "Is that like the Federal Reserve?" or, at best, "How is that different from the Federal Reserve?" Discussion of the credit system works its way around to the inevitable: "Where does the money come from to pay the credit back?" Everything is thought of within the world and assumptions of the current monetarist system. By the time one gets to the Fourth Law, one has usually used up the attention span of the person on the other side of the discussion.

The Fourth Law: A New Language

If one pays attention to LaRouche's Fourth Law, "Adopt a Fusion-Driver 'Crash Program'," one should be stunned by the next sentence: "The essential distinction of man from all lower forms of life, hence, in practice, is that it presents the means for the perfection of the specifically affirmative aims and needs of human individual and social life." And later, "The healthy human culture ... represents a society which is increasing the powers of its productive abilities for progress, to an ever higher level of per-capita existence."

Needless to say, that is not the substance of discussions in Economics 101 classrooms or in corporate boardrooms. Nor is it only economics or business professionals who are clueless. Americans have no idea how thoroughly crippled they are by the metric of money when they speak about economics. It is like using a chimpanzee's vocabulary to discuss Shakespeare's sonnets.

LaRouche begins to introduce the new language, needed for discussing an economics based on the essential distinction of man from all lower forms of life, in the concluding "stretto" section of the Four Laws article. He says,

Henry Ford

We call it "chemistry." Mankind's progress, as measured rather simply as a species, is expressed typically in the rising power of the principle of human life, over the abilities of animal life generally, and relatively absolute superiority over the powers of non-living processes to achieve within mankind's willful intervention to that intended effect. *Progress exists so only under a continuing, progressive increase in the productive and related powers of the human species.*"

It could also be said: *Profit* exists so only under continuing, progressive increase in the productive and related powers of the human species.

While this concept may be foreign to policy makers, business leaders, and citizens today, it was the essence of Hamilton's great economic writings, and it shaped the mental life of the earlier American System industrialists and manufacturers. Two ideas in Hamilton's writings have always stood out for me. The first is his assertion in his *Report on the Subject of Manufactures*, that the wealth of a nation is not its money, or its land, or its raw materials, or its gold, but rather the productive powers of labor.

Alexander Hamilton

The second, is his organization of the mission of the National Bank. While Hamilton knew that those who invested in the bank would need some kind of return on their investment, and he established revenue streams from taxes and tariffs to ensure those returns, he made clear that the mission of the Bank was not to make a monetary profit. The mission of the Bank was to benefit the nation as a whole. The Bank's investment decisions were to be governed by that, not by the individual profit generated from an individual investment. Yet those properly made decisions would ultimately result in profitability throughout the economy. (Look at China's Public Policy Banks today as an example.)

That was how Henry Ford thought when, in 1914, he decided to pay his workers $5 a day and reduce the workday to 8 hours. The reason commonly put forward—that this meant that his workers would then be able to buy his cars—doesn't add up. Ford had about 13,000 people employed at his Highland Park plant, and even if every one of them bought a car, he would not recoup his outlay. It was about the productivity of labor, not only of his own workforce, but of the nation's. Before the wage increase, Ford had to hire 57,000 men per year to keep 13,000 of them employed. The loss of productivity caused by that turnover was enormous. More significantly, that wage increase forced other manufacturers to improve the conditions of their workers, ultimately lifting up living standards nationally. Now, there was a market for his cars!

Similarly, the common idea that the purpose of the assembly line is to speed up the production process is embedded in the let's-cut-costs-to-make-a-profit world. As described in the biography of William Knudsen (Norman Beasley, *Knudsen: A Biography,* Papamoa Press, 2017), the production genius who went from the Ford Motor Company to the presidency of General Motors, and then to the leadership of Franklin Roosevelt's Office of Production Management at the War Production Board: "Knudsen and Ford each saw the automobile as a product of mechanical skill and not a product of mass production. They saw the conveyor as a carrier of material—nothing else.... The carrier produces nothing. It is a beast of burden leaving the mechanic free to do the work." The worker should not be a beast of burden; he should be freed to use his skills and his mind.

This gets closer to the heart of the matter.

The Machine Tool Principle

The early auto industry was a crucible for scientific and technological innovation. New materials came from increasing mastery over the chemical domain. New mechanical configurations came from applica-

EIRNS/Stuart Lewis

Lyndon H. LaRouche, Jr.

tions of the "least action principle." All of that came from the minds of workers. (In one case, a Ford floor sweeper made a suggestion which lead to a breakthrough. He went on to become the head of a major division.)

This is what LaRouche calls "the machine tool principle," the principle that turns science into true profit. On July 23, 1997, LaRouche spoke on this subject to a Washington, D.C. audience at an *EIR* seminar titled, "War on the British, or, How to Save the Economy":

When you're dealing with science, scientific discovery, when you discover an idea, you've got to prove it, haven't you? You say, I've discovered a solution to this problem. Someone says, well, how can you prove it's true, how can you prove it's right? How can you prove it in nature?

So, you construct what's called an experiment. It's called a crucial, or proof-of-principle, experiment, to prove that nature works the way your discovery says it works. That's called a Machine-Tool Principle. Now, when you take the apparatus, which you used to construct that experiment, you walk into a guy who designs machine tools, or similar kinds of products. This guy, having seen your experimental device—he probably helped you build the experiment—now says, "Look, I can design a whole group of new kinds of products, and new kinds of machine tools, on the basis of this discovery which you demonstrated, by looking at your experiment, understanding your experiment. I can see how to build a whole new class of products and processes out of that." ... And that's the way it works. You combine the development of the mind, with the development of the products and processes, which the mind's discovery of principle has devised. And that's how you produce—that's called scientific and technological progress.

That is LaRouche's Fourth Law, and that is called profit.

As Financial System Folds, Trans-Atlantic Officials Call New Silk Road 'Mortal Threat'

by Harley Schlanger

April 27—An article in the German daily, *Süddeutsche Zeitung*, on April 16, about a request made by bank regulators at the European Central Bank (ECB) to Deutsche Bank (DB), "sent shivers down the spines" of financial observers, according to a prominent economic forecaster. "It was not totally unexpected," he added, "as it is not a secret that the bank has been in trouble for a long time; however, seeing it in print caused a shock." What the newspaper reported is that ECB regulators asked the bank to simulate what a "crisis scenario" would look like, should the bank's capital market and derivatives business be hit with defaults, and asked what would be the cost to complete a "resolution" of its investment banking division. In other words, could the bank cover its losses and still survive, or would it require a bailout, a bail-in, or both, to stay in business?

Left unmentioned in the ECB request is an even bigger fear: If a default at Deutsche Bank were to occur, is there a strategy to prevent it from triggering a domino collapse of the other large speculative banks in the Eurozone, all of which have close trading relations with the bank, as well as portfolios filled with bloated derivative contracts?

How to successfully implement a bank "resolution" under conditions of spreading defaults remains unclear for both U.S. and European banks, nearly a decade after the massive government bailouts prevented a collapse of the major "Too Big to Fail" banks, following the September 2008 Crash. While an increase in capital reserves was mandated, and other—mostly cosmetic—measures were introduced, the speculative practices which caused the Crash of 2008 have not only continued, but expanded, due to injections of fresh liquidity by the "quantitative easing" (QE) policy of central banks.

This policy, from the U.S. Federal Reserve, the ECB, and other central banks, provided trillions of dollars of new liquidity to roll over derivative and other speculative debt, so that banks could keep assets on their books at vastly unrealistic face values, and continue to trade them, even while no effort was made to determine whether or not there were any real underlying value of the assets being held and traded. The result is the creation of the largest debt bubble in history.

The liquidity injected by central banks has allowed U.S. and European banks to report large earnings, and to fuel a new stock bubble, even while the real economy is contracting, and economic growth, as measured even by phony GDP statistics, remains

Deutsche Bank is teetering. Deutsche Bank twin towers shown here.

historically low. This stock bubble, and the debt bubble which fueled it, has enabled politicians and bankers to proclaim the fake news that recovery from the 2008 Crash is complete, and the future is bright. Yet, even while this narrative is being pushed, growing concern is being expressed, even within Trans-Atlantic banking and financial circles, that the economy is heading for an even larger blowout in the near future.

That Deutsche Bank is a subject of ECB concern is not surprising. It suffered substantial losses in 2015 and 2016, and has been hit multiple times with significant fines, including a 5.9 billion euro fine imposed by U.S. authorities in 2016 over its handling of mortgage-backed securities. One of the world's largest banks, it has over 42 trillion Euros in derivative exposures. In 2016, the International Monetary Fund (IMF) called DB the "riskiest bank in the world." On April 8, following a rare Sunday night emergency board meeting, CEO John Cryan was dismissed, as the bank continues to experience falling revenues and its stock price has dropped

30% thus far in 2018.

But the ECB's concern is not limited to problems at Deutsche Bank. In addition to ongoing problems in the Italian banking sector, there is new attention focused on the problems with clearing houses, which supposedly safeguard both parties in derivative trades, insulating participants from the effects of a default. The ECB has demanded new powers over the clearing houses in the United States and Britain, insisting that they collect more collateral from clients and increase liquidity buffers. President Trump's former director of the National Economic Council, Gary Cohn, warned in October 2017 of problems of transparency and liquidity in clearing houses, saying that, as "we get less transparency and less liquid assets in the clearing house, it does start to resonate to me to be a new systemic problem in the system."

His comments added to concerns ECB regulators already had about liquidity problems with clearing houses, which first emerged following the Brexit vote, over fear that clearing houses based in London would no longer be under Brussels' jurisdiction, making euro-denominated derivatives trades by EU traders outside the euro-zone even more risky. The London-based euro-clearing house trade can top a notional figure of $900 billion per day, and considerations from the ECB about reducing or eliminating the use of "non-EU" clearing houses posed a real threat to clearing house operators.

It is not only ECB officials who are uneasy about the present financial situation. While U.S. Federal Reserve officials are projecting an air of calm, the rise of interest rates to nearly 3% in defaults on corporate debt, leading to an increase in bankruptcy filings, which is already occurring. Further, one Fed Governor, Lael Brainard, expressed concern about the stock market bubble, albeit in a mild formulation. On April 2, she said "Valuations in a broad set of markets appear elevated relative to historic norms, even after taking into

Department of Treasury

One Fed Governor, Lael Brainard, is concerned about the stock market bubble.

account recent movements."

'Unintended Consequences' of Cheap Money

One commentator not constrained by Brainard's "Fed talk" understatement of the problem of bonded debt and the stock market bubble, is Nomi Prins, author and former investment banker, who warned in her "Financial Road Map for 2018" that the stock market "will continue to rush ahead on the reality of cheap money supply until the debt problems tug at the equity markets and take them down." The financial and capital market system, she said, depends on "co-dependencies and cheap money policies of the central banks." Stock prices have benefited from more than $14 trillion of QE money, which flowed to U.S. banks. In turn, the Fed and other central banks are now holding more than $22 trillion of bond and other debt instruments, with much of the debt they are holding being of dubious value.

Despite brave talk of "unwinding" these holdings and "tapering" cheap money flows, Prins writes that central bankers know this is a problem, but "have no exit plan."

It would help to sharpen this discussion if Prins and others openly referred to a subject raised by economist Lyndon LaRouche in 1995, when he first presented his "Triple Curve," a heuristic device to explain what he called a "Typical Collapse Function." LaRouche's Triple Curve analyzes the interrelationship between three aspects of an economy, that is, financial instruments, monetary aggregates, and real physical production. He showed that what was called the "new economy" emerging in the 1990s exacerbated the problem he identified in 1971: that the triumph of monetarism in the field of economics in the trans-Atlantic region was driving a deindustrialization, while producing speculative financial bubbles.

When he presented the Triple Curve, western economies were characterized by an accelerating increase of financial instruments, an increase in the acceleration of monetary aggregates, and an accelerating collapse of real physical production. LaRouche said this *is* a bubble economy characterized by a financial system that supports itself by hyper-expansion of financial aggregates while collapsing the physical economy by aggressively cutting back lending to the "less-profitable" real, physi-

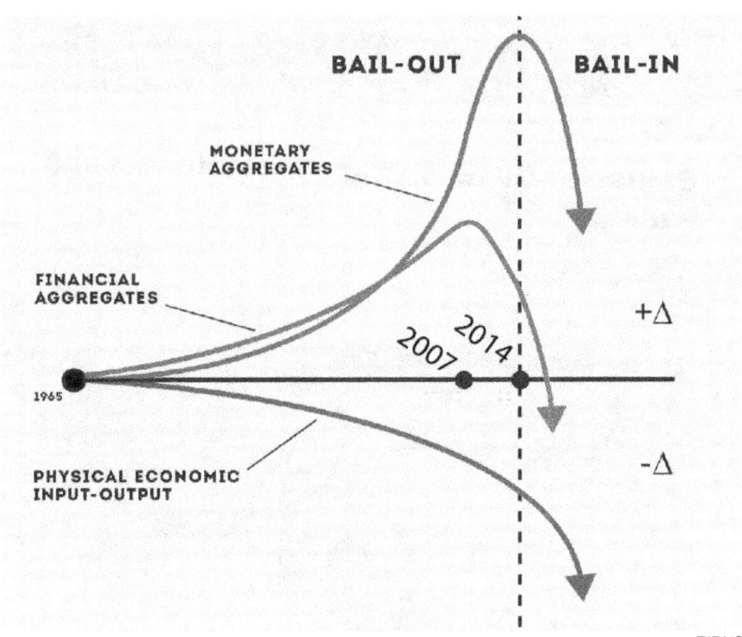

LaRouche's "Triple Curve" Typical Collapse Function.

cal economy.

LaRouche's analysis proved to be accurate in forecasting the popping of successive bubbles, beginning with the Asian crisis in 1997, the Russian GKO bond crisis the following year, the collapse of the dot-com bubble in 2000, and in his July 2007 forecast, of the coming collapse of the mortgage-backed securities bubble. As each bubble popped, hundreds of millions of lives were affected, through an increase in *avoidable* deaths from famine and disease, made worse by banker-dictated austerity measures, and by hopelessness (e.g., the U.S. opioid epidemic) and wars related to economic collapse. The unwillingness to reject such obviously fraudulent monetary theory, which continues to be the driving force of western economies, puts us again on course for a new, even bigger collapse today, LaRouche stated recently.

The growth in all categories of debt is the Achilles heel of the system. Public debt, corporate debt, financial debt, credit card debt, and student loan debt are all soaring, while the means to pay these debts are contracting. In the United States, wage growth and productivity are stagnant, job growth has slowed, and the real labor participation rate (the percentage of those employed who could potentially work) is at a four-decade low. The debt of non-financial corporations in the United States at the end of 2017 was more than $14 trillion, according to statistics from the U.S. Federal Reserve, while corporate profits on average are stagnant or declining. The IMF has estimated that when interest rates hit 3%, more than 20% of U.S. firms will face bankruptcy, as once the ability to borrow is curtailed, interest payments will go into default.

William White, the former chief economist at the Bank for International Settlements, identified the massive flows of liquidity as a new destabilizing factor in finance, which makes all the old models of handling debt useless. In an essay published in April 2018 in the book, *The Changing Fortunes of Central Banking*, he describes this problem as one of "unintended consequences," with today's bailouts adding to future debt, without generating the means to cover the new debts. The failure to address the wild speculation that culminated in the 2008 Crash and bailouts has convinced many CEOs and investors that the only option, in the face of a debt crunch, is to seek ever more risky investments, hoping for a big enough return to cover the spiraling debt costs. He has argued, since 2008, that nothing short of a massive debt write-down can save the system, a point of concurrence with Lyndon LaRouche.

The New Silk Road vs. London

While happy talk about a "robust recovery" dominates public statements from bankers and regulators, and is featured in most media, the fear among financial oligarchs is not only a fear of an uncontrolled collapse in the trans-Atlantic region. Stoking their fears is the emergence of an alternative system in Eurasia, centered around China's impressive New Silk Road global infrastructure development plan, the Belt and Road Initiative (BRI). The growing involvement in BRI projects, on the part of nations in Europe, Africa, and South and Central America, raises the specter of the most feared scenario among those who view the world from the standpoint of classical British geopolitics: that the privileged position held by London-centered banks is about to be eclipsed, and ended, by alliances formed by Eurasian nations with Europe and the United States!

There is an intense economic/diplomatic revolution underway, with new financial institutions, such as the Asian Infrastructure Investment Bank and the BRICS bank, along with large Chinese state and private banks, providing massive amounts of credit for projects. Nations which previously had no option but to subject themselves to looting by London-centered banks, being denied credit, and forced to adopt murderous austerity

Institute for New Economic Thinking

William White, former chief economist at the Bank for International Settlements.

measures, are now turning to this New Paradigm, which China's President Xi Jinping identifies as one based on a win-win perspective. When President Trump showed interest in U.S. participation in the BRI, the neocon/neo-liberal networks in the trans-Atlantic community saw this as an existential threat, which must be countered at all costs, including the risk of new wars.

That is why British imperial interests and their allies have engaged in regime change operations against Trump, launched provocations against Russia and President Putin including the "chemical weapons" frauds of the Skripal affair and faked videos from Douma, Syria, and have made so many hysterical statements characterizing China's development of the New Silk Road as a cover for alleged imperial intentions.

During her weekly webcast, Helga Zepp-LaRouche, founder and President of the Schiller Institute, commented on the rapid consolidation of the BRI, saying that instead of supporting wars against this New Paradigm, its emergence should be embraced by the people of the United States and Europe. "The future of civilization is in Asia, and any country of the West that wants to be part of that future, should find a good relationship to this new dynamic, because this is the forward-looking one, and not the old paradigm as represented by some of these European powers that just think in terms of the past."

This new dynamic, which is taking place in Asia right now, she concluded, "will shape history for the better." The imperial geopoliticians will not like it, but their demise is long overdue.

New Silk Road Resonates with Austria

by Rainer Apel

April 28—An extraordinarily positive development of a growing commitment to the New Silk Road has developed in Austria during the past twelve months. Only a year ago, Austrian relations with China seemed at an all-time low, as petty party interests and frictions had driven the government into a crisis and collapse at the end of April—the direct result being that Austria called off the participation of its transport minister, Joerg Leichtfried, in the Belt and Road Summit in Beijing in mid-May 2017. The cancellation of the China trip by Leichtfried, who had been a strong proponent of his country joining the Silk Road, kept Austrian politics paralyzed until the mid-October early elections. Angered by this standstill in bilateral relations, leading officials of Austrian industry and transport associations launched a strong lobbying for the next government to make a clear commitment to active cooperation with China's New Silk Road.

A week after the Austrian elections, a delegation headed by leaders of the country's national chamber of industry (*Wirtschaftskammer Österreich*, or WKO) and the state railway company (*Österreichische Bundesbahnen*, or ÖBB), left for a several-day tour of China. There, they not only signed a cooperation agreement with their respective partner institutions on the Chinese side, but also stated at press briefings that they expected the new government of Austria to give a "clear priority" to a New Silk Road orientation; otherwise the New Silk Road's enormous dynamic would bypass the Austrian economy.

Remarks such as these, and a big conference of the WKO on the New Silk Road in Vienna on November 21, created the required environment for the two winners of the early elections and coalition partners—the OVP (Austrian People's Party) and the FPO (Freedom Party of Austria) to express a clear commitment to working with China. The official government program of the new coalition partners stated:

Xinhua

Austrian President Alexander van der Bellen (pointing), Austrian Minister for Digital and Economic Affairs Margarete Schrambock (center), and other guests inspect a new China-Europe freight train from Chengdu, China, to Vienna, at the Vienna South Freight Center, April 27, 2018.

Austria lies in the middle of Europe, and thus through its geographic location alone represents an important hub. This position can have an additional enormous benefit from a stronger development of the trans-European networks. We must make sure that big supra-regional and geostrategic infrastructure projects such as, for instance, the planned Silk Road project, or the broad gauge rail project, as well, do not bypass Austria, but that we are a part of it as a hub.

This particularly refers to the extension of the Russian Trans-Siberian Railroad's broad gauge line from Kosice in eastern Slovakia to a huge, new logistics complex near Austria's capital, Vienna—a distance of 400 km. Discussed for many years, this project alone will create 140,000 permanent jobs, but a much broader engagement of Austria's industry and engineering capacities in projects of the New Silk Road in all of Europe's East and Southeast is envisaged as well. This was stated clearly by Johann Strobl, CEO of Austria's Raiffeisen International Bank, who in a year-end interview criticized the EU's China-bashing against the "16

Xi Jinping holds talks with Austrian President Alexander van der Bellen in Beijing, China, April 8, 2018.

plus 1" Summit.[1] He said there is no reason to get alarmed over China's increased role in Eastern and Southeastern Europe: "This is good news. Financial means from outside that flow into Eastern Europe improve the economic potential of the region. Being a bank specializing in Eastern Europe, we are benefiting from that." The EU should change its attitude about China, Strobl added, and "simply face the challenges and find constructive solutions with which the differences in views can be bridged."

China has taken positive notice of these and other recent changes in Austria. During an event on the New Silk Road organized by the prestigious Austrian Society for Traffic and Transport Science (*Österreichische Verkehrswissenschaftliche Gesellschaft*, or ÖVG) in Vienna on January 31, Chinese Ambassador Li Xiaosi directly called on his hosts to make constructive proposals for joint projects, and to even join the "16 plus 1" format, turning it into a "16 plus 1 plus Austria." In response, a spokeswoman for the Austrian foreign ministry said that the Chinese proposal would be carefully studied, once presented officially, but that for the time being, Austria would remain a very close observer of the "16 plus 1."

The first concrete steps in the realization of the New

Silk Road transport connection were made at an international railway conference held in Vienna, February 20-22, during which Russian Railways CEO Oleg Belozerov and Austrian Railways CEO Andreas Mattae signed an agreement for the realization of an integrated Eurasian railway corridor. The 250 delegates to the event, called "Strategic Partnership 1520: Central Europe," included the CEOs of railway companies from 24 countries. An accompanying agreement was signed by the transport ministers of Russia and Austria, Maxim Sokolov and Norbert Hofer, as well.

Under the Russian-Austrian agreements, the parties committed the railway companies and transport agencies of Austria, Slovakia, and Ukraine to construct a new broad gauge (1,520 mm) railway line from Kosice (Slovakia) to Vienna (400 km), including an international logistics center in the twin-city region Vienna-Bratislava. At present, Kosice is the end point of the Russian broad gauge grid. The project is to be carried out by the *Breitspur Planungsgesellschaft mbH*, a joint venture established in 2009 that is registered in Austria, involving Russia, Ukraine, Slovakia, and Austria. This will allow uninterrupted rail freight service from the Kazakh-Chinese border to Central Europe on the Russian broad gauge, with an annual capacity of one million containers, with freight trains reaching a frequency of several hundred weekly. The logistics hub realization alone will create up to 140,000 jobs and spark broader industrial and economic initiatives along the new rail route, creat-

---

1. The "16 plus 1" format is an initiative of the People's Republic of China, aimed at expanding its cooperation with 16 Eastern European and Balkan countries. The initiative was launched at a summit held in Warsaw, Poland, in 2012.

ing more than 600,000 jobs. Concerning the funding of the about 7 billion euros required for the broad gauge extension, Austrian Transport Minister Norbert Hofer also hinted that "investors from Asia" will be interested in the project, which will be completed by 2033.

The central plenary session of the Vienna conference proceeded under the theme, "Eurasian Corridor and New Silk Road. Towards Each Other." Participants discussed ways to achieve higher interoperability between the Chinese and European standard gauge (1435 mm) and the Russian broad gauge (1520 mm). Austria's railway CEO Andreas Matthae said at the Vienna event:

kremlin.ru

Austrian Chancellor Sebastian Kurz.

BMEIR/Angelika Lauber

Austrian Foreign Minister Karin Kneissl.

"The further development of the Eurasian Railway-Landbridge will not only make sure that Europe and Asia come closer to one another, but will also boost economic progress in the participating regions." Matthae has been one of the leading proponents of Austrian constructive cooperation with China's New Silk Road strategy.

Alexander Misharin, First Deputy General Director of Russian Railways, said in Vienna: "The Project OBOR [One Belt One Road] will not only consolidate a unified gauge in the transport systems . . . and promote the emerging of a united Eurasian economic area. The cooperation with the ÖBB is an important step toward a cooperation beneficial for both sides, for the industry as well as for the population of both countries."

In his concluding speech at the Vienna conference, Clemens Foerstl, CEO of RailCargo Austria AG, a freight subsidiary of ÖBB, declared: "We are glad to note that the New Silk Road and the extension of the broad gauge railroad to Vienna are not seen as two different projects, but rather as the common objective to advance Eurasian rail transport. Austria welcomes and supports the development of rail infrastructure in the Eurasian corridor. . . . The Russian-Austrian agreement is a milestone in our efforts to establish the Eurasian Transport Corridor." A follow-up conference was announced for Sochi (Russia) to be held in June 2018.

Austria Steps Beyond the EU

The commitment of the Austrians to step beyond the boundaries of EU geopolitics and enter a new paradigm of international relations became visible March 27, when the government of Austria refused to expel Russian diplomats over the Skripal incident. In a March 28 interview with OE1 radio, Austrian Foreign Minister Karin Kneissl invoked her country's historical tradition of acting as a bridge between East and West, implying that Austria would not expel diplomats, as they are urgently needed right now to solve political issues among countries. The Austrian "no" was all the more justified, she said, as no hard evidence had been presented in the Skripal case, and that even if Russia's blame were to be proved, Austria would "most likely not change views on the matter."

A few days later, Austrian Chancellor Sebastian Kurz explained in an April 4 talk show broadcast on Puls4 TV that he, together with Kneissl, made that decision, "since we traditionally maintain good relations with Russia, are a neutral country, and act as the headquarters for many international organizations such as [an office] of the United Nations and the Organization for Security and Cooperation in Europe. . . . Every day hundreds of diplomats hold talks in Vienna, on neutral territory, and we develop our role in building bridges." On the eve of her meeting with Russian Foreign Minister Sergey Lavrov in Moscow on April 18—a meeting profoundly disliked by the geo-politicians at the EU and NATO—Kneissl reiterated views she had stated on March 28.

The Austrian government also thumbed its nose at the EU geo-politicians by forcefully developing cooperation with China, in clear opposition to the EU's stonewalling on the New Silk Road issue. The largest Austrian delegation ever sent to China visited Beijing, Hainan, and Chengdu, April 7-12. In addition to Austrian President Alexander van der Bellen and Chancellor Kurz, four cabinet ministers (foreign affairs, economics, transport, and environment) joined the delegation of 170 businessmen, 30 academicians, and representatives of the culture sector. That van der Bellen was also an honored guest speaker at the prestigious Boao Forum in Hainan, at the conclusion of his China visit, illustrates that bilateral relations between Austria and China have reached an all-time high.

Foreign Minister Karin Kneissl who, before joining the newly elected government, published a book last September on the rapid rise of China in world affairs, titled *Changing of the Guard*, stated in interviews with the Chinese media that her talks during this trip would not only take into account the role of the Chinese as global investors, but also their increasing importance as political players internationally. Kneissl is known for addressing the inflexibility of the EU's concept of "Europe." In her book, she provocatively writes that young Europeans should enroll at Chinese universities, rather than remain in Europe, since only in China could they really hope to learn something for the future.

Austrian Transport Minister Norbert Hofer—signing a memorandum of understanding with his Chinese counterpart on their common interest in completing the rail corridor from the Greek Mediterranean sea port of Piraeus to Austria's capital Vienna—proudly declared April 10 that his country was "a first mover in Europe" for cooperation with China. To complete the rail corridor, two sections via Hungary and Macedonia must be built.

Symbolizing the new quality of cooperation, the Austrian delegation also attended the ceremony seeing off the first direct freight train departing Chengdu April 12 with Vienna as its destination.

Silk Road of Music

The China tour of the Austrian delegation also featured a high emphasis on culture, philosophy, and music. On the first day of their stay, they were given a special tour of the Confucius Temple in the Forbidden City in Beijing, where the official heritage of the philosopher's contributions is engraved in stone pillars. It was here that Chinese emperors would spend the first hour of their days with ceremonies and meditations, seeking inspiration for a day of good government.

Also on April 10, China's *Fosun* Group and the Vienna Boys' Choir (*Sängerknaben*) signed a cooperation agreement that envisages a vast expansion of proj-

The Vienna Boys Choir performing.

ects in classical music education in numerous cities of China. The agreement, constituting a virtual "Silk Road of Music," was signed in the presence of visiting Austrian President Alexander van der Bellen.

Following an earlier "Silk Road" tour of the Choir ten years ago, about which a feature length film, *Silk Road, Songs Along the Road and Time, with the Vienna Boys' Choir*, was produced on their performances, Vienna's musical input into China has continuously grown, surpassing the intensity of contacts that had existed since 1992. Gerald Wirth, President and Artistic Director of the Vienna Boys' Choir, has been giving classes to Chinese youth in many parts of China during the past several years, always insisting that the training of one's voice is not only good for the development of the individual person, but also for the improvement of society as a whole, because singing ennobles the human character.

Ping Gong, Executive Director and Senior Vice President of the *Fosun* Group, agrees: "Music—and in particular singing—is an essential part of human culture. Singing connects peoples." In this context, the Vienna performance ten years ago of the opera *Mulan* (Magnolia) by the Beijing Opera, featuring Peng Liyuan, the wife of future Chinese President Xi Jinping as a leading soprano, was recalled vividly, not just by the Austrian delegation, but also by the President's wife. As the home and working stage of Haydn, Mozart, Beethoven, and Schubert, Vienna is viewed by many Chinese as the "world capital of classical music." Next to specialized machinery and high-tech products, classical music will be an important cultural heritage exported by Austria to—and shared with—China in the future.

Wieczorek on Ballot as Independent for U.S. Congress in South Dakota

by Marcia Baker

May 1—Ron Wieczorek, a rancher from Davison County, South Dakota, is now on the ballot as an Independent for the November election for South Dakota's one seat in the U.S. House of Representatives. Wieczorek filed with the Secretary of State's office in Pierre on April 24. For several months, he has led an organizing campaign, gathering nearly 4,000 petition signatures with the help of volunteers, and rallying people to get active. He declared in a statement issued for the filing, "I have decided to run for U.S. Congress because I cannot sit idly by while our nation is destroyed. We are sitting on a financial bubble which is about to explode again. Our once productive economy has all but been destroyed by Wall Street's implementation of a post-industrial society and the casino economy, creating a small class of the super-rich and the rest of us. Our infrastructure is crumbling and every financial scheme to repair it presently proposed involves robbing Peter to pay Paul."

Wieczorek's purpose and policies were quite accurately reported in the Pierre *Capital Journal* of April 24: "It's a candidacy based in part on support for President Donald Trump, who Wieczorek says 'has been trapped by partisan politics.' Tuesday afternoon, in the Capitol just outside the Secretary of State's office, he described himself this way: 'I'm a Roosevelt Democrat and an Abraham Lincoln Republican. But neither party seems to know what that is anymore. That's another reason I chose to run as an independent.' " In his campaign statement, he explained, "I choose to stand above the parties and campaign and fight on principle. If the silent Americans who unexpectedly elected Trump and want him to succeed, follow my stance and join me in campaigning on the principles of LaRouche's Four Laws, we can actually cause the necessary changes in time to save our nation."

EIRNS/Bob Baker

Ron Wieczorek briefs the media at the South Dakota Secretary of State's office, April 24, 2018, upon filing.

Wieczorek showed the media the flier he has circulated in the thousands throughout the state, which features the "Four Laws" of emergency measures needed in the nation, outlined in 2014 by Lyndon LaRouche; charts showing the decline of the U.S. farm sector and general economy; and the reason why the United States should join up with China's "Belt and Road" development drive and rebuild our continent. He asserted, "Our nation's elites continue to involve us in purposeless wars, and would, presumably, annihilate the human race to save their system. Our schools long ago ceased to emphasize fundamental discovery, science, and engineering. The people of the 1930s sacrificed and boldly innovated to change a collapsing economic system at that time. They gave me a future. I am repaying that debt of sacrifice by running for Congress to give a future to my grandchildren."

On a conference call with activists the night before

his petition filing, Wieczorek thanked "everyone who put an effort into this campaign," saying, "I have talked to thousands of people—maybe 3, 4, even 5,000 people—in the last two months alone." The process, he said, has shown him that "there is a major improvement in the mindset of people in South Dakota." He spoke of what he will do next: "I'd like to tour the entire state. During the petitioning phase of my campaign, we put out a flier and a card, with Lyndon LaRouche's economic program and the major infrastructure projects we need, and we've touched on the necessity of classical education and music in our

EIRNS

Campaign volunteers with Ron Wieczorek (dark glasses) in South Dakota, April 23, 2018.

school system. We got out, I'm guessing, 5-7,000 of those fliers. We're going to tweak that flier a bit, reprint it, and just keep on circulating it and talking to people.

"I'm looking at this now more as an educational process than an election process, because if we can't educate the American people about what needs to be done, sending me to Washington or even winning the campaign isn't going to solve the problem; but if we can get the people moving, and get them activated, then we can look for a win-win situation, where we'll have a change in our national policy, to get this nation back on track, with Lyn's programs and the American System."

Wieczorek, with his wife Deanna, operates a Charolais breeding herd. He described the hard logistics during his petition drive. "Being out in the farm sector, it's a little different from being in town—20 inches of snow, and we're in the middle of calving season out here. But everything seems to have worked out. The good Lord must have sent some guardian angels to guard us—seems that way to me. My health—He's preserved my health for some reason. At 75, I probably shouldn't be doing this. But nobody else out here is doing it, and it needs to be done. So like they say, Moses didn't go to work 'til he was 80."

Wieczorek is well-known in the farm belt for his decades-long fight for sensible economic policies and principles. He ran three times for South Dakota's Congressional seat in the 1990s (1992, 1994 and 1998), the last time garnering 23% of the Democratic Primary vote. Wieczorek has campaigned vigorously for the platform of development put forward by Lyndon LaRouche, who in 1992 won the North Dakota Democratic Primary for Presidential candidate. Then in 1996, LaRouche placed strongly in many Democratic Presidential primaries around the nation, with 34.5% in North Dakota that year, and significant votes in other farm states—12.7% in Oklahoma and 11.2 in Nebraska and Colorado. However, in 1999, the action LaRouche had warned against, was unfortunately taken by the Federal government: The 1933 Glass-Steagall Act was repealed. More and more "casino economics" came into play, destroying people's lives, to the point of the present-day crisis.

On farm policy, Wieczorek stresses that the Glass-Steagall law should be re-instated, and speculation and trade practices based on a policy ruled by "somebody has to lose and somebody has to win" should stop. He told the *Capital Journal* that the "American political economic system that promoted production agriculture, and the uplifting of human beings with a classical education, teaching our young people how to solve problems in the school system, educating their subconscious, instead of turning them into fodder for these predatory capitalists as cheap labor," is what has to be done.

He told the media and his supporters, "The President's effort to change the established order has been hampered by an outrageous coup conducted by our elites, in conjunction with the British, to change the results of the 2016 election and maintain their system. I am dedicated to ending that coup."

Universal Lessons from China's Advancement in Agriculture

by Mei Fangquan

This is an edited transcription of a July 7, 2017 presentation (English translation) in New York City, by Mei Fangquan, Professor at the Agriculture Information Institute, and Chief Expert of the United Nations Global Food Security Committee, China.

Professor Mei's presentation focused on the success of agriculture in China since 1978. At the time, he and a delegation of Chinese farm and food specialists were attending a July 10-19 United Nations High Level Forum, addressing "Eradicating Hunger," which is the second goal of UN Agenda 2030. China is in the lead internationally, not only for its record of eradicating poverty, but for its example of agriculture advancement.

During that visit, Prof. Mei also spoke July 7, at a Schiller Institute co-sponsored event in Manhattan, titled, "Food for Peace and Thought—China-U.S. Agricultural Cooperation," which was attended by an audience of friends of the Schiller Institute, including people from the U.S. Farmbelt.[1]

Prof. Fangquan described the process of how a sequence of structural adjustments undertaken in China over the last 35 years, has upgraded its farm and food system. This process was further discussed at the October 2017 Communist Party Congress, which ratified three goals, now under implementation: (1) by 2020, the institutional framework is to be in place for maintaining productive and fair agriculture and ecological

Prof. Mei Fangquan

practices; (2) by 2035, there will be "decisive" progress in the agriculture sector; and (3) by 2050, the agriculture sector will be strong and "beautiful," and farmers will be well-off. Aspects of the Chinese experience are now under study and application in Africa, Asia, and South America.

In contrast, in the United States, during the same time period since the 1970s, there has been a dramatic de-structuring of agriculture. The principle of sovereign responsibility for farming and the food supply was set aside, in favor of Wall Street-serving practices of commodity speculation, outsourcing key parts of the food supply, and blocking any provision of fair, parity-based, prices for the farmer's output. Farm counties have been depopulated; infrastructure is decaying; and rural areas suffer from high rates of poverty, suicide, and drug abuse. The average farm family is losing money, and must depend on off-farm jobs to continue to farm.

Thus, when it comes to the heated topic of trade relations—as is now under discussion between the United States and China—the real question of principle must be addressed: what is the government doing for its own people and economy to begin with, and how can win-win trade measures further mutual development for all concerned.

In New York, Prof. Mei welcomed this approach, calling for "joining hands" in promoting positive "agricultural structural adjustments." He and his colleagues conferred one-on-one with the American farmers present, and took a tour of a Hudson Valley dairy farm, hearing first-hand about the U.S. dairy sector

---

1. The conference in New York City, July 7, 2017, was sponsored by the Schiller Institute, the China Energy Fund Committee, and the Foundation for the Revival of Classical Culture. Prof. Mei spoke through an interpreter.

Twenty-five Chinese agricultural specialists joined by nine U.S. farm representatives visit Shenandoah Farm, in Duchess County, N.Y., July 8, 2017, hosted by brothers Verne and Wayne Jackson, whose family has owned it since 1892.

crisis. This month South Dakota rancher Ron Wieczorek, who participated in the New York Schiller event, declared as a candidate for the U.S. House of Representatives, supporting the policy of collaboration with China, to end "the British free trade system" and benefit everyone. (See article on page 24.)
—Marcia Merry Baker

It gives me great pleasure to participate in such an important forum. I was asked to talk about the development of agriculture in China, and lessons and experiences in the process. [**Figure 1**] This is completely different from the topic I had yesterday, and that is why I made different slides for this presentation. I would like to share with you China's strategic and structural changes in its agricultural sector in the last 30 years. I would like to share with you the experience of China's agricultural transformations and organization process. Over the past few years, the central government has been promoting supply-side reform, and that has translated into strategic reforms in the agricultural sector. In the past few decades there have been three major structural changes in the sector in China.

Big Population, Limited Resources

A few words about the basic situation in China. [**Figure 2**] The Chinese population increased from 963 million in 1978 to 1,383 million in 2016. China's population grew really rapidly

FIGURE 1

FIGURE 2

population, resources and environment in China

Item	population	arable land	irrigation area	forest coverage	surface water resources
	0.1 billion	million Ha	million Ha	(percentage)	Cubic metre/capita
1978	9.63	99.4	45.0	12.5	2921
1990	11.43	96.0	47.4	13.2	2460
1995	12.11	95.0	49.4	13.5	2322
2000	12.78	128.2	51.7	15.0	2163
2005	13.08	122.0	55.2	18.2	2076
2010	13.47	92.6	55.7	18.5	1967
2020	14.0-14.1	91.3	57.3	22.0	1826
2030	14.9-15.1	90.0	60.0	25.0	1728

Note: The figures of arable land for year 2000 later are revised according to the joint investigations by FAO and China in 1998

FIGURE 4

Development analysis on major foods consumption in China
中国主要食物消费的发展分析

Year	Country	Grains	Meats	Eggs	Aquatic	Milks	Fruits	Vegetables
1995	China	232	29	11	11	4	32	144
2000	China	206	25	12	12	7	35	139
2010	China	183	29	15	17	25	40	128
2020	China	173	35	18	21	40	45	120
2030	China	140	35	20	24	60	50	120
1990	Japan	125	28	15	40	63	44	114

Note: unit : Kg.

FIGURE 5

Future Goals for Food Development in 2020

Grain: Total production about 620 million tons in 2020 (610-2015)

About 450 kg/per capita

Main Food Consumptions (kg/ per capita):
Meats 35   Eggs 18   Aquatic 21   Milks 40
Fruits 45   Vegetables 120

in the first 20 years after 1978, and after that we have seen a decrease in [the rate of] population growth.

China has limited resources. Looking first at water resources, water resources per capita are one-fourth of the world average, while the arable land per capita is only 40 percent of the world average.

In order to feed over 1 billion people, China is faced with many challenges in terms of resources. [**Figure 3**] It is projected by many different methodologies and many conferences, that the Chinese population might reach its peak in 2030 at 1.6 billion. The current projections say that the peak is going to happen at 1.5 billion. That is the consensus of many departments and academic institutes. Currently we have a population of 1.3 billion, and we believe that every year the population is going to increase by 70-80 million and finally will reach the high point of 1.5 billion.

China's arable land, because of this strict policy, is not facing a sharp decrease. China's irrigation system is relatively developed, while its forestry coverage in the past 10 years has seen rapid growth, because China has stopped destroying forests and is using many alternative materials.

China is faced with scarce water resources, and water resources per capita are decreasing. By 2030, the per-capita water resources will be 1,700 cubic meters per capita. Currently the annual consumption of the U.S. consumer is 2-3,000 cubic meters per capita, so you can see how scarce the water resources in China are.

Now let's look at food consumption in China [**Figure 4**]: By 2025 to 2030, major food consumption in China per capita will peak and will stabilize, as the model projects. The per-capita number, as well as the overall number, will not increase, and we're going to see only structural changes. By that time, we will have a structure similar to that which Japan established in the 1980s.

The only difference will be aquatic products. In fact, the percentage of aquatic products in China was much lower. About 85 percent of aquatic products in Japan are from the high seas. But in the past in China, the supply is different, because we do not have many aquatic products coming from the high seas; 70 percent of them are cultured, which means that we will have to invest in food as feed. Compared with other agricultural countries such as Japan, we are in a completely different situation.

In general, we have an Oriental model of food consumption which is different from the Western model: In terms of meat and poultry, we're not going to see a high percentage in our food mix. In the future, our main target is to ensure food supply. [**Figures 5 and 6**] Our second target is to ensure the quality and safety of our food. These are our two major targets.

In the future, by 2020, total agricultural output will reach 620 million tons, while per-capita production is going to be 450 kg per capita. The major food consumption projections were already shown in a previous table. [**Figure 4**]

In 2015 total agricultural food output had a value of $1.8 trillion; by 2020 it's going to be $2.3 trillion. We are the country with the biggest food industry, but we do not have a very strong industry, because we do not have a large number of multinationals.

Here are a number of very important figures about China's agricultural structure [**Figure 7**]: In 2015, 40 percent of food production was used as animal feed. By 2030, half of China's food output will be used as animal feed. Many countries and many people are not familiar with such a structure: They assume that food is mostly consumed by people in China, but that is not true.

Three Strategic Agricultural Reforms

Now a few words about the history of major structural changes in China's agricultural development in the past 30-plus years. We call them "strategic" changes because they happen every 10-plus years; we see major changes in investment, input/output strategies, policies, etc., and we see them change once every 10-plus years.

The first reform was between 1979 and 1988. [**Figure 8**] In 1978, total grain production was 300 billion kg. In 1984, total grain production reached 400 billion kg. The per-capita amount was 400 kg: That reform solved the problem of feeding most of the Chinese people.

After reaching the per-capita amount of 400 kg, we were faced with the problem of selling surplus grain, because in the history of China, lack of food was always the problem. But by 1984, we had achieved a grain surplus, and that is why the government needed to make further changes. [**Figure 9**] The first policy was to promote coordinated development of food crops and cash crops. The second was to support cotton, oil, and other economic crops. And in the development of the third, the government allowed part of the grains to be used as feed to support the development of animal husbandry. In the past, before solving the problem of feeding the population, Chinese people did not actually have access to a lot of meat, poultry, eggs, or milk.

The second reform [**Figure 10**] took place between 1998

FIGURE 6

Goals for Food Industry

In 2015 total output value of Chinese food industry reached 1800 billion US dollar.

By 2020, It will reach 2300 billion US dollar.

FIGURE 7

By the years 2030, 50% of the total grain demands will be used as animal feeds.

Proportion of feed grain
in total grain

Year	Proportion
1980	8%
1990	21%
2000	33%
2010	38%
2020	43%
2030	50%

FIGURE 8

The first agricultural structure
adjustment (1979-1988)

1978 total grain production 300 billion kilograms

In 1984 the total grain production reached 400 billion kilograms, 400 kilograms per capita for the first time and it solved the food and clothing problems

FIGURE 9

Major adjustment measures:

- **Promote the coordinated development of food crops and cash crops**
- **Support cotton and oil and other economic crops to accelerate development**
- **Part of the grain as feed to support the development of animal husbandry**

and 2003. In 1998, total grain output reached 500 billion kg for the first time, representing a second wave of grain surplus. Because of the high inventory, the government adopted a number of additional reform measures. At that time, the ecology was degrading, so the government also adopted policies to return some farmland to forests, fishery sites, or husbandry sites.

This reform resulted in significant improvements in the Chinese agricultural sector [**Figure 11**], reducing pressure on the land and the environment, as well as the agricultural and ecological environment. And there has been a significant improvement in China's agricultural structure. In the past 10-plus years, forestry coverage has increased very rapidly. If you look at western and northern China, over 10 years ago you could barely see *any* greenery, if you traveled in the area. Now in some areas, these places are covered by forests. That is a result of government reform.

But these policies back then led to a decrease in grain output from 500 to 430 billion kg. When a new administration came into power they saw that the grain inventory was under stress, while output was under pressure as well.

That's why the new administration launched the third reform. [**Figure 12**] By 2015, grain output had seen growth for 12 successive years, because of the government's favorable policies and an increase in imports. In 2015 our grain output reached 600 billion kg for the first time. We saw three increases: first, food production increased; second, food stocks inventory increased; and third, food prices increased. The three increases meant that a third reform of structural changes was needed.

Usually you have to have a big picture, because importers would be interested in importing food without looking at food's historical output, and that is because back then, management of the agricultural sector was siloed.

Starting in 2016, a strategic reform was implemented to deal with the problem of very high corn stocks. [**Figure 13**] Because of too much corn on the market, the price dropped, and that is why a large amount of corn is used as animal feed.

The third reform, therefore, aimed at using corn to feed animals and [support] husbandry instead of people, because of the corn surplus. Seventy percent of corn output in China is now used as animal feed, because of the policy changes. Currently the government is trying to deal with the large inventory as well as change the ways corn is planted, but that is not going to solve the problem fundamentally, if corn continues to be used as a major source of animal feed.

In the 1990s, we conducted two projects, one in the south and one in the north of China. We discovered that if we replaced the corn grown for human consumption with corn for animal feed, we could increase the efficiency by 30%, which means that if the arable land decreases in size, the efficiency in output will not decrease concurrently.

So, we have to accelerate the pace of building a sustainable system that combines agriculture and animal husbandry which is sustainable.

Organic vs. Green

After this policy was adopted, a new target for the development of the agriculture sector included the following [**Figure 14**]: The ultimate goal is to establish a modern, efficient, ecological and organic sector—a modern agricultural sector, that will use resources efficiently while protecting the environment.

While these three elements are very important, so is the development of green products, the steady development of organic products. Many people have been talking about organic products in the past two days. But the price of organic products is much higher than that of conventional products. Germany was the first to develop organic products. But the share of organic in Germany is not big, because of the high prices. We have to focus more on the development of *green* products, instead of *organic* products, which will carry the brand label "green base." We have to develop green industrial chains.

In the meantime, we have to put in place a modern ecological industry. Ecological development is very important; the whole eco-system has to be protected. [**Figure 15**] We cannot simply make big investments to improve the environment; if we do so without producing anything, we might be under pressure. Ecological protection and industrial development must proceed hand in hand, at the same time.

In the meantime, China is witnessing rapid development in combining its big health sector, tourism, agriculture, and the recreational sector. We use the "Three P's" model: That is, the combination of public investment and social capital against the backdrop of a decrease of investment in major industries. Investment in big health industry has been constantly growing. This is conducive to the development of the big health industry that combines agriculture, tourism, and recreation.

Agricultural structural adjustment is the inevitable process of agricultural progress and modernization. [**Figure 16**] Every adjustment constitutes an upgrade to a higher stage of development.

After the first stage of restructuring, we became successful in feeding our population. The second restructuring focussed on the reuse of land and reforestation. And the third restructuring put in place a modern feed system, combining ecological protection and industrial development.

Let us join hands in promoting the agricultural structural adjustments! Thank you. [applause]

FIGURE 13

From 2016 the corn acreage began to reduce, as well as the corn production and inventories.

Must be accelerated to be used for feed corn gradually adjusted for the feed,

Create conditions to convert 70% of corn into feed crop.

FIGURE 14

Explore the Development model of modern and efficient ecological agriculture

Focus on the development of modern and efficient ecological agriculture

Focus on the development of green food

Solve the problem of organic matter circulation in ecosystems

Brand --- green base

FIGURE 15

New development goals of modern agriculture:

Dual goals:

Protect the ecological environment rational use of resources

Speed up economic growth and change the mode of development

Realization: modern --- efficient --- ecology - organic combination

FIGURE 16

Agricultural structural adjustment is the inevitable process of agricultural progress and modernization

Every adjustment is an upgrade, into a higher stage of development.

BEYOND TOMORROW: SUDDENLY, IT'S ALL OMINOUS!

The History Just Ahead

by Lyndon H. LaRouche, Jr.

December 24, 2013

With yesterday's announcement, that the U.S. intention is to move U.S. Army combat capabilities more forcefully into the Pacific theater, the combination of military forces appears to have committed both Pacific and Atlantic "frontal" forces to the early prospect, of a general thermonuclear-armed, global war, one conducted by the increasingly, desperately bankrupt, so-called "allied forces."

This occurs under the condition that the economy of the trans-Atlantic alliance, has just greatly accelerated the dive into physical bankruptcy taken by the trans-Atlantic powers, while the now emerging economic alliance of north and central Eurasian nations, is moving steadily into a coalition of sovereign governments, a coalition intended to be achieved by the time of the close of the immediately coming year.

The foreseeable circumstances of the immediately on-coming new year are, momentarily, such, that if U.S. President Obama's de-facto current dictatorship retains power in the U.S.A., the Anglo-Dutch imperial forces will tend to maintain a postured commitment to thermonuclear warfare, against the nations of northern Eurasia, done within increasingly aggressive postures, and probable early deployment. The consequence of such a posture, would probably be an early extinction of the human species. Actual thermonuclear warfare under

---

This is the third of three related works by LaRouche that appeared in the Jan. 10, 2014 issue of *EIR*. We reprinted the first, "Science & the Solar System," in our April 27, 2018 issue. We are not currently reprinting "The Promethean Method To Save Civilization Today," which was an address given by Mr. LaRouche on January 3, 2014, which may be read at http://www.larouchepub.com/lar/2014/webcasts/4102wbcst_jan_3.html

present capabilities, threatens to be like that.

Were Obama to be removed from office quickly, the U.S.A.'s tendency toward abandoning the Anglo-Dutch scheme, might become a serious, if not certain likelihood. Then, the medium-term perspective, might be the development of policies of constructive peace, and of ultimate economic recoveries among the greater part of the global nation-state authorities.

However, in the meantime, the bestialities of the Anglo-Dutch imperialism, may be quieted, but remain to be also quenched. In any case, "we must work at it," as a likeness of the late U.S. President Franklin Roosevelt would have done, had he not died when he did.

I.

The Subject of the Global Oligarchical Principle

It will have been, hopefully, recalled, during the recent past days of this now passing December 2013, that the only serious hope for humanity, is that U.S. President Barack Obama will have been recalled from duty, that for excellent and urgent reasons, and, that the consequent revival of the souls of the U.S. population, will prevent the presently lurking threat of the human species' thermonuclear extinction.

That now still-threatened outcome of the months ahead, could, and must be, immediately blocked and soon prevented; otherwise, it were even probable that "people were soon no more." The British Queen's already ongoing commitment to the extermination of about six billions persons out of the presently estimated seven, is already no longer merely threatened intentions; rather, the continued reign of President Obama in the United States, has also been "upgraded" to a massive increase of the death rate within the present U.S. population, during this present new year: unless he were soon removed from office. That is already a virtual U.S.A. legislative fact. Most among the Republican leaders, so far, seem to be insane in this respect, while most Democratic leaders appear to be seriously confused on this matter at this same time: an unleashing of the Democratic members of the Senate from the inclinations of what is, ostensibly, their present overseer (or, should we say, "whip,") might be considered most helpful on this account—by some. Unfortunately, since the final illness of President Franklin Roosevelt, true courage against attempted tyrannies, has not been a strong point among either our own present political leaderships, or, also, even many ordinary citizens.

What I have just stated, in these immediately preceding paragraphs, contains no exaggeration by me. The question to be addressed to me, is, "how do we kick the relevant motor into starting? Where has the relevant 'political guts' been hiding itself?"

For useable answers, we must emphasize some crucially important recent facts, facts respecting the relative rise in power of a relatively large part of the main body of the Eurasian nations, nations which are now largely apart from the already ruined regions of Southwest Asia. There has been a gradually accelerating physical-economic strength, coming to the surface of trends in principal regions of Eurasia, that in sharp contrast to now highly accelerated declines in western regions of Europe and, in particular, the rapidly accelerated collapse of the economy of North America, the United States itself, most notably. The murderously disastrous ruin of the U.S. economy, is the most important factor in the fostering of the feasibility of the presently threatened, possibly very earlier outbreak of a global thermonuclear extermination of the human population. The presently rapid, virtually utter loss of the former agro-industrial ability of the United States, has been the

"Unfortunately," writes LaRouche, "since the final illness of President Franklin Roosevelt, true courage against attempted tyrannies, has not been a strong point among either their own present political leaderships, or, also, even many ordinary citizens."

most notable economic and general strategic factor in the entirety of the recently accelerating threat of a sudden outbreak of planetary thermonuclear warfare.

There could be no competently historical insight into this crucial factor—the U.S. factor—of the span of the recent and future history of the crisis which I have indicated here this far, without taking into account my own active part in the wave of the most crucial part of the history of the world since the passing of President Franklin Roosevelt.

It had all begun, in effect, at least, with the last moments of President Roosevelt's life, as the OSS chief had then just recently departed from his last meeting with that President. By the time that my continued military service had transported me to India, I had found myself politically engaged in mourning the death of President Franklin Roosevelt, and, at the same time, finding myself uttering the working equivalent of a solemn dedication to the continuation of the mission of President Franklin Roosevelt, all that in opposition to the hateful political image of the newly cast President Harry S Truman. It was the taste of treason already prophetically embedded in everything that Truman was then, and later, which had stirred me, during those times, to a permanent dedication to the cause which Franklin Roosevelt had embodied immortally in my mind. I shared, in that memory, a rich memory of the wonderful former President John Quincy Adams' living out of his own dedication to the future of our United States, and had felt the strong hand of President Franklin Roosevelt's commitments, as an echo of President Washington, and of Alexander Hamilton's murder by the British royal butcher, Aaron Burr, and of, notably, Presidents and the most American political martyrs-in-office, Abraham Lincoln, William McKinley, and John F. Kennedy.

That fact, as known to me throughout the course of the ensuing decades, is what stirs my devotions to the future of all mankind, now, still, actively, today. It is not merely my memory; it was, and is a still-living, very active insight into the meaning of the ground of history through which I continue to walk, to walk as a still actively living active participant in the process which is the shaping of the Presidency of our United States and its mission for mankind. Those who had once known better than I had now later come to know, are presently given only the rarest of presently possible alternatives, that of the role of a qualified, still-active trustee of my own assigned devotion to the future of both our republic, and of mankind in a larger way. I encounter the effect of what is becoming now the fullness of a solitary reality, one of which I am most frequently, and most passionately reminded daily, since the retirement of the former President Bill Clinton from the Presidency, and from President Franklin Roosevelt's Glass Steagall Law, alike. To know current history, one must live it, that done in a certain fullness of a life-long experience.

That much, which I have just stated, is indispensable; I think I need add no more than that, in particular, for the moment.

II.

Making the Future Now

On the condition that that much said in the preceding chapter, were already taken into account, we are freed to turn our attention to the future; it is done for that purpose, which should begin by looking backwards toward the outcome of what had been a successful peace among the nations: the actual future. The expressed practical aspects of the intentions now in the process of their design, must be clearly defined before attempting to explain why and how that result might be brought about.

By their nature, true leaders are those who have acquired that virtue of an experience which is foreseeing the future missions of mankind's rise to what could and must be done, as also I have done for my part. Most of our species, presently, have lost an effective insight into the making of the future; they dwell in the drudgeries and monotonies of a bare, and often bleak experience, rather than the creating of the necessary future as such as Nicholas of Cusa and his followers in science had done.

At present, there could be no actually competent, scientific approaches to this challenge as a present one, without taking into account the essential distinction be-

> **Most of our species, presently, have lost an effective insight into the making of the future; they dwell in the drudgeries and monotonies of a bare, and often bleak experience, rather than the creating of the necessary future as such as Nicholas of Cusa and his followers in science had done.**

tween the human species and forms of essentially animal life. That distinction is truly elementary, only when it is stated in precisely those terms, as I have summarized the elementary distinction in an earlier publication, to the following effect:[1]

The Human Principle

Although, conventional opinion places the identities of Zeus and Prometheus, as characters confined to an ancient Greek mythology, the physical evidence of the chemistry expressed, is, that "Prometheus" is the name given to the model of a once actually living creature identified and equipped with the actual origins, and characteristics from which the origins of modern physical scientific practices are to be traced, historically, to the origins of the principle of human behavior based in the ever-upward evolutionary features of the origins of the practice which is, in turn, the unique quality of the ostensibly willful mode of upward evolutionary progress of the chemistry of the human species, a chemistry which has been uniquely specific to the relevant effects of the willfully induced effects which, in turn, are dependent upon the continuing evolutionary developments produced by the process of applied, anti-primitive modern chemistry. The avowed principle of the Prometheans, is their determination of true scientists to overthrow those intrinsically evil, intrinsically and viciously, and culturally stupefied and brutishly immoral, oligarchical cultures, such as those of the ancient Roman Empire, of the butchers who murdered the Trojans, and, who are the currently avowed devotees of the radically practiced "population-reduction" policies, of such as the British empire's current Queen Elizabeth II, and of the current U.S.A.'s "Greenies" associated with the pro-genocide measures of that political class whose

---

1. Prometheus vs. Zeus, in Lyndon H. LaRouche, Jr. "Back to Genesis," in <u>Science and the Solar System</u>, December 9, 2013, in the January 24, 2014 issue of *EIR*.

current has been recently set into motion, again, by the "Hitler-resembling" practices prescribed by the presently current decrees and other legislation of President Barack Obama.

The practical emphasis on the facts of the matter, must be placed genetically, exactly so.

Any doubt respecting my emphasis on the biological effects, pertains essentially to voluntary choices of members of the human species as such. Hence, the necessity of the precise Classical representation of the history of the opposition between the followers of Zeus, and those of the actual current candidates for association with the name of "The Prometheans."

To Wit!

Actually, even the often so-called "greenies" could not have existed without a biological origin in the relevant sort of depraved characteristics of the human breed. We should perhaps emphasize the term: "It's in the breed!" No actually practicing, true human being would deny a notion of biological necessity of upward evolutionary biological progress of the human species *per se*. It is to be strictly emphasized, that biology *per se,* has no natural basis in necessity of breeding as such; the determination of the development of the human individual is intrinsically voluntary, not otherwise simply biological. The development of the children of Zeus, on the other hand, is the product of a moral degeneration conditioned within the personalities and communities composed of those who share a disposition for the manifestations of the oligarchical type; they are the products of an acquired, diseased, or simply depraved pathology, not a biologically natural predisposition for the true progress of mankind.

Healthy modes of human cultural trends, are not "naturally" related to oligarchical characteristics of behavior. The point was demonstrated in the achievements of the culture of the so-called Golden Renaissance of such as Filippo Brunelleschi and Nicholas of Cusa. The prevalent mass-depravity incident during most of the following century demonstrates the expressions of the oligarchical influences of the enemies of Cusa and his legacy, a legacy including the generation of the Seventeenth-century period of the achievements of the Massachusetts Bay colony prior to its crushing by the evil Dutch tyrannies and by the later emergence

The destruction of Troy (12th/13th Century B.C.) is the archetype for the brutal population-reduction policies of the oligarchy, typified today by the British royal family and its greenie shocktroops. Shown: Jan Bruegel the Elder, "The Burning of Troy" (1621).

of the intrinsically mass-murderous practices of the British empire through to the present date.

Similarly, the case of Thomas Jefferson's disgusting departure from the original Presidency, and of the British monarchy's official murderer Aaron Burr, typify the various mere scoundrels, such as the renegade Thomas Jefferson of his wicked days, on the one hand, and his sometimes sympathetic rival and accomplice, the British hired murderer, Aaron Burr on the other, who was the sponsor of both U.S. Presidents Andrew Jackson and Martin Van Buren, the latter a pair of a type bred from the environs of British-banker scoundrels of the British-banker riddled New York City region of the United States.

For a clearer insight into these matters, contrast the type of those British bankers and their likeness, to that actually United States' principle of national banking which had been created by the same Alexander Hamilton who was the actual founder of the economic system of our originally constituted United States. The principle of U.S. banking's founding, was not the exchange of money as merely money, but, instead, the physical-economic values of the goods produced and exchanged at an appropriately prescribed, rising track in physically relative values of exchange as such. ***The Glass-Steagall law established by the actions of President Franklin D. Roosevelt, echoes and typifies, thus, the standard of the original U.S. Dollar. Money-per-se has no intrinsic such value.*** (Hamilton had made the distinction perfectly clear.)

The notion of an intrinsic value of a monetary standard of exchange, depends, typically and intrinsically, on the increased physical value, per capita, of the U.S. dollar as such. In other words, a steady increase in the physically productive powers of labor. Money *per se* could never be an honest measure of value *per se*. The honest value of labor could never be anything but the increase of the physical benefit to humanity's population, by the means of the increase of the effect of the physical increase, for mankind, of the physically productive powers of the productivity of *the human intellect* which drives the benefit of human labor upward *per capita*. It is the expression of a perpetual human productivity-in-fact, not money, which defines true economic worth for mankind.

That is the measure of *the future* of mankind. But, the future of mankind has a higher purpose than any man's mere greed; that subject is the next chapter on the agenda of this report.

III.

The Value of the Human Species

The value of the human species resides in its successfully, and successively upward creations. In simple terms, this means the increase of the physical level of mastery of the processes within our Solar system (for example), as those may be measured in mankind's increasing authority in the development of the accessible aspects of our proximate, upward reach within the Solar system. Convenient practical terms of reference for this purpose, were also laid down since approximately the 1890s, this time in terms of those higher expressions of energy-flux density associated with the consequences of the progress set into motion presently by the work of such as Max Planck and Albert Einstein. Thermonuclear fusion's practical development is a conveniently approximated reference for the time being; the recent discoveries reported by China's success in its landing on the Moon, have now suddenly become a standard of reference for current practice, with the subject of matter-antimatter lurking around still.

The more commonplace sort of practical approach to the subjects at hand among me and my relevant associates, currently, is the effective energy-flux density approach to achieving missions inclusive of those by man within Solar space, especially relatively nearby space (if only for the next moment waiting ahead).

The human standard for measure of the same achievement, is located in the realized experience of the human being regarded in its terms of being a species. The quest for a higher achievement within human reach, is our most convenient standard.

That much said now on that account; the needed perspective is the perpetual commitment to achievement of the next one of the still uncompleted, "impossible" accomplishments available in foresight ahead.

The needed perspective is the perpetual commitment to achievement of the next one of the still uncompleted, "impossible" accomplishments available in foresight ahead. This subject of "foresight," is extremely troubling for the mere oligarchs; their shriveled imaginations are fixed on the subject of "money". . . .

This subject of "foresight," is extremely troubling for the mere oligarchs; their shriveled imaginations are fixed on the subject of "money," when the real issue is the urgency of accelerating mankind's power to progress far beyond.

What is clear to those relevant persons among us presently, is that the foolishness of the children of Zeus, has put the human species, repeatedly, perilously behind what should be regarded, respected, and also feared, as representing a great risk to the continued existence of our human species. For example: the prospect of a fatal encounter of our human species with some satellite of one sort of another, should have been already worrying serious scientific thinkers for quite some time.

The implications of such foolishness as evasion of that threat, must be considered thoroughly on that account. Such is the proper measure of the practical value of the particular human creature in view of our nearby celestial habitats.

The 'Brutish?' Monarchy

The key to the present global crisis of mankind, is to be located, most typically for today, by the actual role occupied by the name of the present British monarchy, its predecessor-in-principle, and by its extended, earlier, and prospective future, expressions, as the modern heir-apparent of the original evil typified by the reality and image of the *Zeus*, who is otherwise identified as the enemy of *Prometheus*. The particular, rarely under-

www.news.cn

The recent discoveries reported by China's success in its landing on the Moon, has now suddenly become a standard of reference for current scientific practice. Here, China's Chang'e 3 rover, Yutu (Jade Rabbit), explores the Moon's surface, Dec. 15, 2013.

stood significance of those names, is that they were known under those names, as nothing differing essentially from certain real personalities and the principles by which they are identified-in-fact of still-contemporary realities, as a matter of still-contemporary practice. For example, the nominally "British Empire," was never anything differing in characteristics from the cult of the original *Zeus*.

These have become customarily identified as mythological creatures; but, that is intrinsically a systemic quality of modern customs of misrepresentation.

The actual expression for the principled characteristics of the incarnate evil of the character named "Zeus," is the name given to an archetype attributed, as in the relevant ancient Greek sources, to the original principle of human evil otherwise known to modern society as *"the oligarchical principle."*

As a somewhat clarifying matter of fact, the term Zeus, is presently a name for interchangeably-named organizations of societies whose systemic characteristic, and whose actual legacy have been what is typified in fact as "the oligarchical principle." The particular significance of that title, is not that equivalent to the ordinary notion of "king," or a simply defined "kingdom." The convenient modern term of description, would include the title of "emperor." The Roman Empire typifies the legacy of a kind of super-Zeus, as the relevant example from the **Iliad**, and its included genocide against the population of the mass-murdered citizens of the ancient city of **Troy**. The British Empire, as currently still extant, is the now customary model of reference for the currently modern history of our planet.

Thus, for example, the present form of the Saudi kingdom and its specific accomplices, are all an integral part, currently, of the British Empire under the present monarchy.

The particular, actually practical implications of such classifications from among the roster of forms of social organizations among humans, or the like, fits more or less exactly with the traditional meaning of the supposedly merely mythical figure of *Zeus* and his court. The implications differ very little from the recent classification of the U.S. unemployed under the just recently installed status of derelicts created by U.S. President Obama's prescriptions for the treatment of the "long-term unemployed." Cannibalism could be a variant of that same policy.

More immediately notable, is the policy of the currently nominal successor to Zeus, the currently, nominal Queen of England, who expresses a mimicking of the Queen of England's influence on President Barack Obama's policies toward the "long-term unemployed" U.S. citizens, by the Queen's demand for the reduction of the entirety of the current human population of Earth, from a recently approximate seven billions living persons, to something in the direction of less than one billion for the entire human species. Her stated intention on that account, illustrates the reality of the presently expressed aim of a rather immediate launching of a world-wide thermonuclear war in the prospectively very near term. The evidence is already in the process of implementation, and the Queen's active Saudi minion-dom is a currently most notable feature of both the general process afoot and its well-known advent in the so-called Anglo-Saudi "9-11" operations, just as the related actions under both U.S. Presidents George W. Bush, Jr. and, now, Barack Obama, fill such roles.

Those immediately preceding considerations are essential facts, with respect to identifying the systemically defined implications of the legacy of the Zeus-versus-Prometheus matter and its implications for not only the world, but also much of the Solar system, presently.

Next: Zeus vs. Prometheus

The foregoing information respecting the Zeus-principle, prepares the ground for addressing the necessary references which I have presented immediately above, as to the implications of the reference to the mere name of Zeus. Now, our attention is turned to the "hard facts" of this present publication's facts, in its proper entirety, and the necessity for the preceding aspects of this report as a whole. The evidence which I shall introduce from this point of the current report, onwards, goes directly to the most crucial among the practical features of any actually competent presentation of the elementary principles of a competent study of modern economy.

IV.

Prometheus vs. Zeus

The actual existence, role and importance of the original concept of Zeus-versus-Prometheus, has no different basis in ancient Greek customs than the difference of man *Promethean*) from the actually human degenerates which are better identified as bestialized man. The crucial evidence is both the combined existence and progress of living mankind, and the viciously anti-humanistic (so-called "Green") characteristics of the degenerate forms of practice associated with a growing spread of modern imperialist systems and other systems characteristic of anti-human practices, such as those of the ancient Roman empire (in particular) and such nominally British and related imperialist cultures associated with the legacy of the notions and customary characteristics of imperialist systems.

The characteristics of modernized versions of systems consistent with the tradition of Zeus, are associated with what is precisely identified as the oligarchical system's characteristics in general, and the particular example of the degenerate practice still taught and known as Euclidean geometry, as distinct from a true, modern, physical geometry.

The distinction of a modern scientific practice, from degenerate forms familiar from many pre-Renaissance European cultures generally, stems from the beginning of modern European science of the Renaissance of such as the scientific achievements associated with the modern physicist Filippo Brunelleschi and Nicholas of Cusa, and of Cusa's own, inspired followers such as Johannes Kepler and those whom both Cusa and Kepler

"The followers of Zeus, are, intrinsically, self-doomed to a probable species-extinction in the presently looming, nuclear-warfare-like prospects for the future of mankind." Shown: Zeus with his eagle and thunderbolt, Athenian red-figure amphora 5th Century B.C.

had more or less directly inspired. However, the medieval tradition of relatively, historically outstanding actual science among human cultures had been reached earlier, on a grand scale, leading into pre-Renaissance and later modern engineering, with the exceptional achievements in economics and grand-scale engineering developments specific to the hitherto massive accomplishments of the work of Charlemagne in logistics and economy.

The most relevant feature of post-Renaissance scientific progress had been set into motion by such as Brunelleschi and Cusa, with Cusa actually the most outstanding of them all respecting the breadth and depth of his combined work and its consequences. These specific considerations, when situated in the setting of Cusa's part in the process, have been, if considered in retrospect, the most influential in the consequences of their accomplishments. That much now said in necessary preparations, we may now proceed freely to the specific goal of our intentions in this present report taken as an entirety.

The True Advent of Chemistry

Truth to tell, I admit now my now very rare, but still occasional glimpses of my continued harboring of a 1942 edition of what had been long the standard **Handbook of Chemistry and Physics**; but, without rejecting the merits to be recognized from later editions of that reference-work, there is a systemic error in the choice of the context which that customary approach to physics and chemistry, as such, had both neglected to consider, the actual role of the human mind and its living actuality as such. Here is where my part in the history comes most directly into play, as I shall now do as indicated.

The issue is the choice of the proper definition of the chosen subject matter. Are, for example, both chemistry and physics as such the actual subject, or are they not merely products of that which creates the discovery, the products which are the actually unique powers of the development of the process which is the human mind as such? Do you think that that is merely a fair description for purposes of polite conversation; or, is the human mind as such, to be considered the organ which produces the existence of good practices of chemistry? I present the case for the latter choice of principle.

Do you propose to punish the particular mind which fails to perform as prescribed? (A common academic practice! For example.) Or, should you not place the emphasis, not on the chemistry as such, for example, but, instead, let the mind develop itself, to assume the direction of the process? (That could cut out most of the worse-than-pure-waste of funding the now customarily utterly worse-than-wasteful appetites of stock-brokerages.) What, therefore, is the challenge to society now to be set before us?

This now takes our present discussion to the core of the matter being considered in this study and report as a whole: how does mere chemistry actually take over, also on behalf of the human mind itself, rather than the lower-ranking league of such as the mere U.S. Federal NSA?

The Little-Known Mystery of Actually Thinking

How could you know, with certainty, when the mind may actually not be thinking something which can be somehow unknown to the watching observer? That presumes that interventions of the type classifiable under the heading of externally applied torture of the mind of the intended victim are excluded, either mechanically or in a related fashion. Or, how does the torturer know

who to torture for what purpose? In other words, presume we exclude the Adolf Hitler-style stuff. For example: how could you torture the guy you can not identify for torture? By now, you have pointed the finger to the alternatives used by the Adolf Hitler regime and comparable cases. That brings all of the crucial issues into play; in other words, the same old oligarchical system typical of the infamous Zeus.

That is, essentially, exactly what and why Zeus did it.

Does that mean that the issue is Zeus' methods of conditioning virtually mere slaves by means of actual or implicit mental torture? No; the issue is whether or not society will permit the existence of what can be considered an actually human quality of performance extracted from terrorized or like cases of some form of effective slavery, as by throwing Christians to the lions. The result, as the Romans demonstrated at the end of the torturing and murdering of Christians, for example, is what are fairly described as "dehumanized" human victims of such regimes as those, for example, of U.S. Presidents George W. Bush, Jr. and, most emphatically, the currently incumbent Barack Obama.

That consideration, now properly considered, brings us to the actually experimental subject of the demonstrable difference between the conditions under the reign of Zeus's torture, and the creative mentality of the followers of Prometheus. The followers of Zeus, are, intrinsically, self-doomed to a probable species-extinction in the presently looming, nuclear-warfare-like prospects for the future of mankind.

V.

The Missions of Prometheus

Sometimes, like good American citizens, we support and relish the life of being American citizens, for example, as all really good American citizens do; what we prize is the freedom of that citizenship, which I admire, and my adversaries such as George W. Bush, Jr., and Barack Obama manifestly do not. That, in itself, is an important point of great merit, in and of itself; but the subject requires us to look much, much deeper.

The essence of the subject-matter, is what is often identified as "freedom," particularly what has been sometimes graciously known as typically American freedom; in particular, the freedom expressed by the brief existence of the Massachusetts Bay Colony before it was crushed by the Dutch mass-murderers of that century, and, later, the same tyranny was continued under the rubrics of the so-called "British" imperial system which continues to dominate the greatest single region, in subjected area, of that actual world empire up through the present date.[2] The Hitler regime was, from its actual beginning, originally a branch of the British imperial system, and that pretty much from the start, until the Winston Churchill bunch had decided it to be smarter to bring in the United States under President Franklin D. Roosevelt, with aid of certain British who thought that President Roosevelt was not scheduled to remain in charge of the United States for much longer after 1939. The death of President Roosevelt was used as the means for the crushing of the policies and practices of what had been the Roosevelt administration. The so-called Americans associated with then Hitler-associate Prescott Bush, played a crucial role in the process which included the convenient crushing, under President Harry S Truman, of everything essential in what had been the post-war intentions of President Franklin Roosevelt.[3]

The election of President John F. Kennedy until his assassination,[4] which had since been arranged to ensure that no one would be permitted to continue to live without coming under a very efficient degree of control over the associates and offshoots of the likes of Prescott Bush. If you wished to be President, thereafter, crawl before Wall Street and London, and a place might be arranged for you. The witting submission of much of the Federal system's reigning authorities, showed the truth of the matter, in the role of both two-term President George W. Bush, Jr., and, now, British puppet Barack Obama in their occupation of the U.S. Presidency.

The time has now come, when the mischiefs from such pasts as a U.S. Government whose best Presidents were usually assassinated, can not be tolerated by the human species any longer. The new mission of Prometheus must be brought forth, promptly, now. The present crisis-situation demands it.

"The new mission of Prometheus must be brought forth, promptly, now," LaRouche writes. "The present crisis-situation demands it." Shown: Prometheus takes fire from the gods, to bring to man, by Jan Cossiers, 17th Century.

The Principle of Prometheus

The principle of Prometheus, separates his identity from that of all presently known human oligarchs and oligarchies, alike. The following is the essential distinction of principle, of fully human persons, from the intellectually deformed, otherwise human victims of the quality of slavery which imitates lower forms of life. *That is the essential point of distinction, of Prometheus from the children of Zeus.*

The functional distinction which separates the two opposing categories in a fully systemic respect, is matter of mental distinction of the two *apposite* types, as finger from thumb of the same original breeding of the living stalk. The reduction of the actually human individual to a slave, is precisely a typical such distinction. The difference in type of behavior, and of the consequences of that distinction, is also the essence of the distinction of both slaves and also of slave-masters (the accomplices of Zeus), from what may be fairly identified as the Prometheans.

The most essential feature of that just-stated point of distinction, is the crucial point of emphasis to be addressed here. It is the effects of that in-bred distinction

---

2. For example: the Saudi kingdom is essentially a satellite, like other subjects of that same empire, as we should have discovered from witnessing the so-called "9-11" murder of American citizens by the joint means organized under the funding and preparing of both the British monarchy and the Saudi kingdom.

3. Essentially, the U.S.A. under Truman, had been a project of the British monarchy's supervision, in conjunction with what had always been British-controlled Wall Street operations in banking since the roots of Manhattan and the scoundrels who exploited the crushing of the original New England settlements.

4. Sponsored by the widow of President Franklin Roosevelt, Eleanor Roosevelt, who had been the only effectively residual authority left alive following his highly successful Presidential leadership. John F. Kennedy was the last U.S. President who enjoyed an authority free from the legacy of the Anglo-American crew associated with the associates of the London-rooted role of Prescott Bush, and his off-shoots.

between the two types from common human origins, which is the location of the distinctions between the two apparent types. The root of the functional difference is an effect of the distinction of the creative human personality, as a type, from the willing slave. That is the core of the Promethean principle, the difference in principle of behavior of the child of Prometheus, as distinguished from the slave-mentalities which are to be associated with the notion of the qualities of the relatively systemically degraded victims of the contamination which is characteristic of the prevalent influence of the Zeus-influence.

The essentially functional distinction between the two contrasted *functional* types, is what is often identified as "intellectual." The one is creative, or "intellectual;" the other, is merely "practical." The root of that distinction can be defined as shown to be *precise*. However, the expression of the relative degree of distinction, which defines a greater degree of difference between the "creative" and "merely practical," is the locality of the distinction of relatively free persons, from those who are conditioned to submission to behavior characteristic among slaves. Such is the rule-of-thumb sort of distinc-

tion of a mental state of serfdom, and that of a person identified as animal-like bondage as slaves.

The crucial issues of distinction among the varying types which might be reasonably attributable, point to, above all, the expression of voluntary creative mental powers, in varying degrees of expression as such. The crucial quality of distinction among those exhibiting talents of active creativity, is found in those persons who have successfully cultivated the qualities of mental development of what is to be classed as scientific and related qualities of creativity comparable to those of great Classical musicians and what fall, otherwise, into both actively creative physical scientific discoverers of true physical principles, and artistic creativity of a comparable, but distinct expression of the same quality rightly identified as "genius."

It is those persons who have been advantaged by the development of what is usefully identified as genius, who demonstrate in practice the relative qualities rightly dubbed "genius." The proper intention of society, is to cultivate the development of all human individuals into an expression of the principle of such "genius."

FIDELIO

Journal of Poetry, Science, and Statecraft

From the first issue, dated Winter 1992, featuring Lyndon LaRouche on "The Science of Music: The Solution to Plato's Paradox of 'The One and the Many,'" to the final issue of Spring/Summer 2006, a "Symposium on Edgar Allan Poe and the Spirit of the American Revolution," *Fidelio* magazine gave voice to the Schiller Institute's intention to create a new Golden Renaissance.

The title of the magazine, is taken from Beethoven's great opera, which celebrates the struggle for political freedom over tyranny. *Fidelio* was founded at the time that LaRouche and several of his close associates were unjustly imprisoned, as was the opera's Florestan, whose character was based on the American Revolutionary hero, the French General, Marquis de Lafayette.

Each issue of *Fidelio*, throughout its 14-year lifespan, remained faithful to its initial commitment, and offered original writings by LaRouche and his associates, on matters of, what the poet Percy Byssche Shelley identified as, "profound and impassioned conceptions respecting man and nature."

Back issues are now available for purchase through the Schiller Institute website:
http://schillerinstitute.org/about/order_form.html

REPORT FROM GERMANY

German Government on the Slippery Slope: Blank Check for Breach of International Law

by Helga Zepp-LaRouche, Chair of the German political party
Civil Rights Movement Solidarity (*BüSo*)

April 28—When the Berlin government unhesitatingly supports the military aggression against Syria, knowing that it would be considered a breach of international law by the Scientific Service (*Wissenschaftliche Dienste*) of the Bundestag, the alarm bells should go off. Mrs. Merkel characterized the air strikes by the U.S., Britain and France—which were carried out even before investigations could be made into whether chemical weapons were even used, and if so, who was responsible—as "necessary and appropriate." And the Minister of Defense, Ursula von der Leyen, reaffirmed Germany's willingness in principle to participate in future such aggression, saying "What Great Britain contributed from the air, we can also perform. However, we were not asked this time."

The expert opinion of the Scientific Service, released on April 18, characterizes the military strikes of the 14th of April as a clear breach of international law.[1] They were a relapse into the pattern of military interventions called "reprisals" in the period prior to the First World War. In assessing them from the standpoint of international law, the opinion notes, it is even more significant that the allied military did not wait for the OPCW inspections. Nor did the recent aggression differ fundamentally from the attacks already carried out by the United States alone in April 2017, which were unanimously considered to be contrary to international law.

The principle of international legality, the experts found, was thus abandoned in favor of a subjective "political-moral legitimacy," which in turn constitutes a violation of the prohibition of force under international law (Article 2 No. 4 of the UN Charter). Thus, the air raids were a blatant return to a form of armed reprisals—believed to have been vanquished by international law—but this time in "humanitarian" garb.

Such reprisals—also known as gunboat diplomacy—used to be common practice before the First World War, and occasionally between the wars. After the terrible catastrophe of the Second World War, they were banned under international law, as set out in the UN Charter.

There was neither an issue of self-defense nor a decision taken by the UN Security Council, the opinion states, and only the United Kingdom laid out its own legal position in a policy paper of April 14, 2018.

In this paper, the British government sets out the typical argument for "humanitarian interventions," as we have known them since the 1999 Blair Doctrine. The Scientific Service commented: "The British legal position on the military strikes against Syria, which Germany has apparently backed in principle, is unconvincing in the final analysis." The British approach, it

---

1. See https://www.bundestag.de/blob/551344/f8055ab0bba-0ced333ebcd8478e74e4e/wd-2-048-18-pdf-data.pdf

continues, merely represents another "variety" of the legal concept of so-called "humanitarian intervention" without a Security Council mandate, and of the concept of "responsibility to protect" ("R2P") under international law. Because of the risk of abuse, it explains, the admissibility of humanitarian intervention is extremely controversial in international law, and does not appear valid as an exception under common law to the prohibition of force under international law.

We would just add to that, that Article 26 of the Basic Law [Germany's provisional constitution] prohibits a war of aggression and makes such preparation a criminal offense. But the implementing law required for this article (Art. 80 StGB) has been suspended since January 1, 2017—by the same Merkel government![2]

Lawyer Andreas Kulick of the Eberhard Karls University in Tübingen points to another fatal consequence of a relapse into the era of reprisals. If western alliances violate international law and instead use subjective moral criteria as pretext for military intervention, every country in the world could in principle use that as a precedent for military aggression against any others.

But what is the deeper reason for this scandalous behavior of a German government which takes positions as though there had not been a history of the Twentieth Century with two world wars?

After all, it is not only that German Defense Minister Ursula von der Leyen was aware of the report of the Scientific Service of the Bundestag; one can also assume that she knows the historical and strategic background of the tragedy of the Near and Middle East. During the mid-70s, Zbigniew Brzezinski played the "Islamic card" against the Soviet Union, without which there would never have been the radicalization of Islam. In the decades since then, various geopolitical forces of the West have used the Mujahedin, Al-Qaeda, Al-Nusra, or the Islamic State (ISIS/ISIL/IS), to name but a few, in support of "good" Islamists vs. "evil" ones, in order to impose regime change on governments that opposed the idea of a unipolar world.

It can't have escaped the attention of the Defense Ministry that former U.S. Defense Intelligence Agency (DIA) head General Michael Flynn accused the Obama administration, in an interview with *Al Jazeera* of July 29, 2015, of having built up ISIS deliberately, and not as a result of a miscalculation.[3] The intention behind this, he said, was to build an "Islamic caliphate" on the territory of Iraq and Syria. In May of that same year, in the context of an FOIA lawsuit, Judicial Watch obtained a DIA memorandum from 2012 containing the analysis that the U.S. had weapons from Qaddafi's arsenals shipped to the Syrian rebels, with the same intent, i.e., to build an Islamic caliphate. The DIA reports were the basis on which then U.S. Chief of Staff Martin Dempsey was able to prevent Obama at the last moment from carrying out the planned military strike against Syria in September 2013. It would be very strange if General Flynn's insights had nothing to do with the reason he became the first victim of the attempted coup d'état against President Trump, staged by MI6 and the secret service heads of the Obama Administration.

Former British diplomat and secret agent Alastair Crooke commented on Flynn's allegations about Obama in a November 13, 2015 article on the Conflict Forum website: "No one wanted to touch the 'live wire' of possible U.S. collusion with Caliphate forces. But it was clear enough what the American General was saying: the jihadification of the Syrian conflict had been a 'wilful' policy decision, and that since Al-Qaeda and the ISIS embryo were the only movements capable of establishing such a Caliphate across Syria and Iraq, then it plainly followed that the U.S. Administration, and its allies, tacitly accepted this outcome, in the interests of weakening, or of overthrowing, the Syrian state."

The same view as that of General Flynn—that the U.S. administration had deliberately built up ISIS and was therefore responsible for the refugee catastrophe— was put forth in 2015 by the head of the Russian Republic of Chechnya, Ramzan Kadyrov. He said that he was in possession of information that the former CIA chief and commander of the coalition forces in Iraq and Afghanistan, General David Petraeus, had personally recruited the head of ISIS, Abu Bakr Al-Baghdadi, to work in the interests of the USA. The later head of the Islamic State, who according to Kadyrov was in Petraeus' service, had previously founded Al-Nusra.

The long history of supporting the "good rebels"

<hr>

2. See https://www.heise.de/tp/features/80-StGB-Vorbereitung-eines-Angriffskriegs-ist-seit-1-Januar-2017-gestrichen-3590763.html

3. See https://www.aljazeera.com/programmes/headtohead/2015/07/blame-isil-150728080342288.html

with money, weapons and training by various Western governments against the legitimate sovereign governments of Southwest Asia, is well known. The Obama Pentagon, among other things, provided $500 million to train 5,000 Syrian jihadists, who then joined the terrorist groups.

Incidentally, the tacit acceptance of this policy by the allies is one of the direct causes of the migration which is responsible for the refugee crisis. If Mrs. Merkel wants to fight the "causes for fleeing," as she has at least occasionally claimed she does, then she could start with the guilty entanglement of the West in this policy. It is all the more hypocritical if the Minister of Defense wants to participate in the future in further military interventions, which would only result in further suffering for the affected populations. It is equally abhorrent that the EU and the German government are only willing to participate in reconstruction measures for areas in Syria that are not under the control of the Assad government. So regime change is still on the agenda.

While the German government obviously has no problem in wrecking international law as established after the Second World War, and venturing further along the dangerous path of geopolitics, the nations of Asia are demonstrating what peaceful coexistence for mutual benefit can look like. The historic summit between North and South Korea, which China, the United States and Russia were instrumental in bringing about, as well as the equally important summit between Chinese President Xi Jinping and Indian Prime Minister Narendra Modi, represent the policy of the new paradigm which, unfortunately, the German government is miles away from even understanding.

We urgently need a new policy in Germany!

zepp-larouche@eir.de

The Sociological Return

Methodology & Social Media

Dr Rob Watson